ENCOUNTERS
Chinese Language and Culture

Character Writing Workbook 2

ENCOUNTERS
Chinese Language and Culture

Character Writing Workbook 2

漢字學習本
汉字学习本

Rongzhen Li
Yale University

Unit Introductions by John S. Montanaro
Yale University

Yale UNIVERSITY PRESS
New Haven and London

华语教学出版社
SINOLINGUA

Published with assistance from the Office of the President, Yale University.

Director of Digital Publishing: David Schiffman

Project Director: Mary Jane Peluso
Editor: Timothy J. Shea
Editorial Assistant: Ash Lago
Developmental Editor: S. C. Yu
Project Manager: Karen Hohner
Digital Product Manager: Sara Sapire
Copy Editor: Jamie Greene
Managing Editor: Jenya Weinreb
Designer and Compositor: Daniel Tschudi
Cover Designer: Wanda España/Wee Design Group
Production Controller: Maureen Noonan
Marketing Manager: Karen Stickler

Printed in the United States of America.

ISBN: 978-0-300-16171-7

This paper meets the requirements of ANSI/NISO Z39.48-1992 (Permanence of Paper).

10 9 8 7 6 5 4 3 2 1

Contents

Introduction

Welcome to writing practice. This book is a companion to *Encounters* Student Book 2, and it will help you learn the Chinese characters required for writing. Note that many other characters are presented in the Reading sections of *Encounters*, but these are not practiced here. We practice here only those required for writing recall. Keep in mind that writing and reading go hand in hand, so practice in one leads to increased proficiency in the other. What's more, writing is just plain fun. So give some time to developing a decent handwriting. You'll be proud of yourself and of your Chinese.

Stroke Order: Basic Guidelines

There is usually a conventional sequence in which the strokes of Chinese characters are written, although there does exist some variation among Chinese writers. Diligent practice will soon fix the major principles in your mind. Here are some basic guidelines.

1. Left before right, as in 八 (*bā*, 'eight').

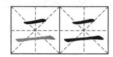

2. Top to bottom, as in 二 (*èr*, 'two').

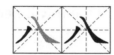

3. Horizontal line before vertical one, as in 十 (*shí*, 'ten').

4. Left-slanting line before an intersecting right-slanting line, as in 乂 (*yì*, 'significance').

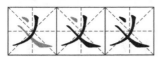

5. Central part before symmetrical sides, as in 小 (*xiǎo*, 'small').

6. Outside before inside, as in 同 (*tóng*, 'same').

7. If the 'enclosure' is complete on all four sides, the last stroke is the bottom one, as in 四 (*sì*, 'four').

8. If the character is framed from above, the frame is written first, as in 同 (*tóng*, 'same').

9. If the character is framed from the bottom, the frame is written last, as in 凶 (*xiōng*, 'ferocious').

These rules will not cover every situation, but they apply to the overwhelming majority of cases. Refer to them often and practice them frequently. Most or all of them will become automatic as you learn to write more and more characters.

A Guide to the Information on Character Sheets

• Boxes: Pronunciation of the character in pinyin, meaning of the character in English, common word or phrase using the character, ancient and later forms of the character, modern traditional form, and simplified form (if any).

xué	Ancient Form	Later Form	Modern Traditional Form	Modern Simplified Form
study; learn; imitate	𦥑	學	學	学
xuéxiào			學校	学校

• Information about the character, including radical, phonetic, memory aid, etc.
   The ancient and later forms of 學/学 both have two hands with sticks used for learning counting, and a house. The later form has a 子 ('child') added at the bottom as the radical since children spend a lot of time learning.
• Usage of the character in words, phrases, and sentences.
   學/学 often appears in compound words relating to 'study,' 'school,' or 'academics.' For example:

學問/学问 study + ask = 'knowledge'	學年/学年 study + year = 'school year'
學期/学期 study + term = 'semester'	大學/大学 big + study = 'university'

這隻鳥會學人説話。	这只鸟会学人说话。
這個學期你要學什麼課?	这个学期你要学什么课?
我想學打毛線。	我想学打毛线。
去年我學了三個星期的中文。	去年我学了三个星期的中文。

• Stroke-by-stroke guide to writing the character; squares for you to practice writing the character.

Modern Traditional Form	Modern Simplified Form
學 學 學 學 學 學	学 学 学 学 学 学
學 學 學 學 學 學	学 学
學 學 學 學	
學	学

Unit 11

The sentences below are inspired by the contents of Unit 11 and contain all the new characters required for writing as well as others. Read and reread until fluent, covering the English as you read. Then cover the English and try to reproduce the Chinese equivalents orally. Do this exercise before beginning to practice writing.

我不知道怎麼回答這個問題。 我不知道怎么回答这个问题。	I don't know how to answer this question.
認識新朋友很有意思。 认识新朋友很有意思。	It's interesting to get to know new friends.
中國人新年見面會說恭喜發財。 中国人新年见面会说恭喜发财。	Chinese people say 'May you be happy and prosperous' when they meet each other on New Year.
他和我是好朋友，我們很談得來。 他和我是好朋友，我们很谈得来。	He and I are good friends; we get along very well.
她很客氣地说：對不起，讓你們久等了。 她很客气地说：对不起，让你们久等了。	She said politely, 'I'm sorry to have kept you waiting for so long.'
老師把問題寫在黑板上讓學生來回答。 老师把问题写在黑板上让学生来回答。	The teacher wrote the questions on the blackboard and had students answer them.
我不愛呆在家裡，我喜歡找朋友一起出去 　玩兒。 我不爱呆在家里，我喜欢找朋友一起出去 　玩儿。	I don't like to stay home; I like to go out with friends.
我問了很多問題，我的新朋友很客氣地一 　個一個地回答了。 我问了很多问题，我的新朋友很客气地一 　个一个地回答了。	I asked lots of questions, and my new friend answered each one of them politely.

Just How Were Chinese Characters 'Simplified'?

Well, first of all, let's remind ourselves that 'simplified' simply means that there are fewer strokes required for writing certain characters. 'Simplified' does not mean 'easier to learn.' In fact, in the view of some learners of Chinese, the simplified variety is harder to learn than the traditional* forms, because the simplified forms appear to have reduced the 'picture' quality of Chinese characters.

That aside for the moment, we think a better understanding of the strategies employed by the reformers of the traditional script can be of benefit to the learning process. If you have already used *Encounters* Book 1, you have had the option of choosing which script, simplified or traditional, to learn to write. You may also have elected the option to practice reading both scripts. If you intend to go further in your study of Chinese, you will likely need to be functional in both scripts. Whichever strategy you choose, we think a clearer understanding of how one got to be the other will help. Here are a few guidelines to the process of simplification.

1. Hundreds of characters were simplified by simplifying the radical, thereby reducing stroke count. Examples:

見	turned into	见
魚	turned into	鱼
門	turned into	门
貝	turned into	贝
金	turned into	钅

2. Hundreds more traditional characters were simplified by changing the phonetic component, so,

歷 (*lì*, 'history')	became	历 (actually providing an easier phonetic mnemonic [力 *lì*])
遠 (*yuǎn*, 'far')	became	远 (again providing a better phonetic)
國 (*guó*, 'country')	became	国 (altering the phonetic 或 *huò* to 玉 *yù*, but thereby providing less phonetic help. *Huò* could, with some imagination lead us to *guó*. Where does *yù* take us?)

---

*Traditional Chinese characters are used in Taiwan, Hong Kong, Macau, and many overseas Chinese communities, whereas simplified Chinese characters are used in the PRC and Singapore. In all of these locations, however, both forms of characters often appear in particular contexts: in Taiwan on publications intended to ease travel for Mainland visitors, and in the PRC as part of ornamental or decorative writing.

3. Others were simplified by retaining only part of the traditional character, so,

電 (*diàn*, 'electricity')	became	电 (but in the process we lost the top component, the character 雨 [*yǔ* 'rain'], so vital in the production of 'electricity'!)
開 (*kāi*, 'open')	became	开 (but again in the simplified form, we lost *mén* ['door'], so important in any 'opening.')

4. Some characters adopted 'simplified' forms already common in Chinese handwriting, so,

車 (*chē*, 'vehicle')	became	车
門 (*mén*, 'door')	became	门

5. Finally, some characters became entirely new characters, so,

幾 (*jǐ*, 'how many')	became	几

And so on, and so on, until about one-third of the entire inventory of Chinese characters handed down through the centuries were altered. But keep in mind that the overwhelming majority of Chinese characters have *not* been changed. Most still have only one form; many have two forms, but both forms are easily distinguished and relate clearly to each other; few have been radically changed, and these are easily learned.

Our advice? As far as writing and reading are concerned, 寫簡讀繁/写简读繁 *xiě jiǎn dú fán* ('Write simplified and read traditional.') Learning both forms at the same time is not equivalent to learning two entirely different scripts: It is learning slightly different forms of the same script, because there is far more convergence than divergence between the two. Moreover, learning to *read* both forms at the same time allows recognition of one form to reinforce recognition of the other. Serious students of Chinese cannot expect *never* to have to read either simplified or traditional characters; there will come a time in their careers when they wish they could read the 'other' format. And, when that time comes, it should not come as a shock; it should not come with a feeling that 'Oh no, I have to start all over again!' The transition should come smoothly and comfortably; students should be prepared for it and not surprised by it.

Our approach in *Encounters* reflects the reality of the Chinese reading world. Throughout the *Encounters* materials, we regard preparing students for the language reality they will face as our foremost guiding principle.

問/问 (wèn)

wèn	Ancient Form	Later Form	Modern Traditional Form	Modern Simplified Form
ask; inquire	問	問	問	问
wènhǎo			問好	问好

問/问 is a picto-phonetic character. 門/门 (*mén*, 'door' [a pictographic character]) is the phonetic component although it sounds quite different from *wèn*. 口 is the radical meaning 'mouth,' indicating that the meaning of the whole character 問/问 is related to 'mouth.' To help you remember, you can associate 門/门 and 口 with the meaning of 問/问 as 'knocking on one's door to inquire.' Distinguish: 同, 問/问, 用, 月, 周, 网. 問/问 appears in compound words relating to 'ask,' 'inquire,' or 'interrogate.' For example:

問題/问题 ask + subject = 'question'	問好/问好 ask + good; well = 'say hello to'
學問/学问 study + ask = 'knowledge'	請問/请问 please + ask = 'Excuse me; May I ask . . . ?'

請問，我能問你一個問題嗎?	请问，我能问你一个问题吗?
你的問題問得很好。	你的问题问得很好。
請問，你叫什麼名字?	请问，你叫什么名字?
請問，這個字是什麼意思?	请问，这个字是什么意思?

Modern Traditional Form	Modern Simplified Form
問 問 問 問 問 問 問 問 問 問 問 問	问 问 问 问 问 问

Copyright © 2012 by Yale University and China International Publishing Group

tí	Later Form	Modern Traditional Form	Modern Simplified Form
subject; title of a composition or speech; inscription	題	題	题
wèntí		問題	问题

頁／页, the right part of 題／题, is the radical. In the later form of 題／题, this radical looks like a person with a big head. In modern forms, this part is written as 頁／页. (頁／页 by itself means 'page,' a measure word for paper.) When it is a component of other characters, it usually indicates that the whole character is related to 'head.' For example:

火 ('fire') + 頁／页 ('head') = 煩／烦 ('upset, troubled')	丁 (*dīng*, 'up' [also a phonetic component here]) + 頁／页 ('head') = 頂／顶 ('top, summit')

是, the left part of 題／题, is the phonetic component. When 是 stands alone, it is pronounced *shì*, meaning 'be.' However, when 是 appears in other characters as a phonetic component, the characters are usually pronounced *tí*. For example: 題／题, 提, 緹／缇, 醍, 鯷／鳀. Look up these characters in a dictionary to find out their meanings.

題／题 originally meant 'forehead.' Later it was extended to mean 'front.' Since a title of a composition or speech is always mentioned up front, the modern meaning of 題／题 is 'title of a composition or speech; subject.' Refer to the following compound words:

問題／问题 ask + subject = 'question'	題目／题目 subject + eye; item = 'exam item'
考題／考题 test + subject = 'exam question'	話題／话题 talk + subject = 'topic'

請問，我能問你一個問題嗎？	请问，我能问你一个问题吗？
這個話題很有意思。	这个话题很有意思。
這些考題太難了。	这些考题太难了。
你們有什麼問題，都可以問我。	你们有什么问题，都可以问我。

Modern Traditional Form	Modern Simplified Form
题 题 题 题 题 题	题 题 题 题 题 题
题 题 题 题 题 题	题 题 题 题 题 题
题 题 题 题 题 题	题 题 题

题

题

Copyright © 2012 by Yale University and China International Publishing Group

tán	Later Form	Modern Traditional Form	Modern Simplified Form
talk; chat	談	談	谈
tántiān		談天	谈天

談/谈 is a picto-phonetic character. The left part, 言/讠 (a mouth at the bottom and some horizontal lines indicating sound waves), is the radical indicating 談/谈 is related to 'speech.' The right part, 炎 (*yán*), is the phonetic component. Since 炎 is made up of two 'fire' characters, think of 談/谈 as 'talking up a hot conversation.' 談/谈 appears in compound words relating to 'talk' and 'chat.' For example:

談天/谈天 talk + sky; weather = 'casual chat'	談心/谈心 talk + heart = 'heart-to-heart talk'
面談/面谈 face + talk = 'interview; speak to somebody face to face'	會談/会谈 meet + talk = 'talks; conversation; negotiation'

你和誰談得來？和誰談不來？	你和谁谈得来？和谁谈不来？
你和新認識的朋友都談了些什麼？	你和新认识的朋友都谈了些什么？
最近我女朋友和我有一些問題，我想找個時間和她好好談談。	最近我女朋友和我有一些问题，我想找个时间和她好好谈谈。
他總是愛談他的寵物。	他总是爱谈他的宠物。

Modern Traditional Form	Modern Simplified Form
談 談 談 談 談 談 談 談 談 談 談 談 談 談 談	谈 谈 谈 谈 谈 谈 谈 谈 谈 谈
談	谈

氣／气 (qì)

qì	Ancient Form	Later Form	Modern Traditional Form	Modern Simplified Form
air; breath; airs; manner	三	气	氣	气
tiānqì			天氣	天气

氣／气 means 'air.' The ancient form is three lines, representing airflow. In the later form, the three lines are curved to be differentiated from the character 三 ('three'). The ancient Chinese associated breath with air. But to have breath, one has to be fed with rice. So a new character 氣 was created, with the phonetic and radical component 气 at the top and another radical, 米 ('rice'), at the bottom. 氣 originally only meant 'to feed.' Nowadays it primarily means 'air' and 'breath.' The modern traditional form 氣 retains the radical 米, but the simplified form 气 reverts back to its ancient form.

In ancient Chinese philosophy, 'air' was an essential element of the earth, and it was also essential for one's spirit. Therefore, 氣／气 often appears in compound words relating to 'air,' 'manner,' or 'spirit.' For example:

客氣／客气 guest + manner = 'polite'	靈氣／灵气 clever + spirit = 'sharp and perceptive'
小氣／小气 small; little + manner = 'petty; stingy'	天氣／天气 sky + air = 'weather'

他太小氣了，我和他常常談不來。	他太小气了，我和他常常谈不来。
我們已經是一家人了，以後不要那麼客氣了。	我们已经是一家人了，以后不要那么客气了。
你那麼有靈氣，學什麼樂器都能學會。 　　—你過獎了。	你那么有灵气，学什么乐器都能学会。 　　—你过奖了。
不管天氣好不好，我都要出去遛狗。	不管天气好不好，我都要出去遛狗。

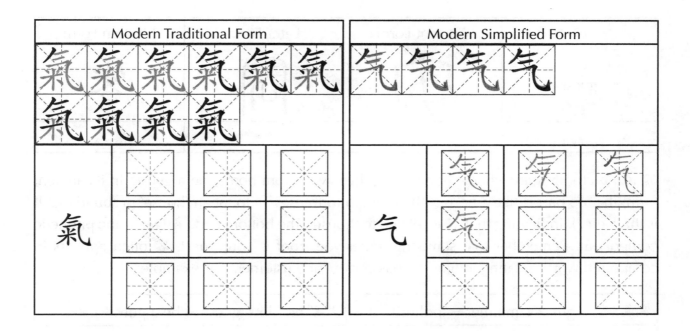

Modern Traditional Form				Modern Simplified Form		
氣				气	气	气
					气	

客 (kè)

kè	Ancient Form	Later Form	Modern Form
guest	窌	窎	客
kèren			客人

客 is a picto-phonetic character meaning 'live away from home; be a guest.' In its ancient form, the top part is like a house. The modern form uses 宀 to mean 'house' or 'building.' It is the radical, indicating that 客 is related to 'house.' The bottom part, 各 (gè), is the phonetic component. Remember that someone under your roof is your guest. 客 often appears in compound words relating to 'guest,' 'passenger,' or 'customer.' For example:

客氣/客气 guest + manner = 'polite'	做客 be; do + guest = 'be a guest'
請客/请客 please; invite + guest = 'treat; entertain a guest'	遊客/游客 travel + guest = 'tourist'

我新認識的那位藝術家，又英俊又客氣。	我新认识的那位艺术家，又英俊又客气。
你發大財了，什麼時候請客？	你发大财了，什么时候请客？
今天我家裡要請客，客人很多，都是我父母的朋友。	今天我家里要请客，客人很多，都是我父母的朋友。
我的寵物狗對熟悉的人很友好，對不熟悉的人就很不客氣。	我的宠物狗对熟悉的人很友好，对不熟悉的人就很不客气。

客 客 客 客 客 客
客 客 客
客

朋 (*péng*)

péng	Ancient Form	Later Form	Modern Form
friend; companion	𨺅	𦰩	朋
péngyou			朋友

朋 is a pictographic character. Its original meaning was the name of a unit of currency. The ancient form of 朋 depicts two clusters of cowries. Five cowries form one cluster, and two clusters form one 朋. Since two clusters of the same cowries form one 朋, 朋 is also used to refer to the same kind of people or things. From this, 朋 was extended to mean 朋友, 'friends.' The modern form of 朋 is written with the radical 月 (*yuè*, 'moon') doubled. Think…of the moon reflected in each of the eyes of your best friend?

他是你的好朋友還是普通朋友?	他是你的好朋友还是普通朋友?
我和新認識的那位英俊的藝術家，很快就變成了好朋友。	我和新认识的那位英俊的艺术家，很快就变成了好朋友。
我有美國朋友，也有中國朋友。	我有美国朋友，也有中国朋友。
我們只是普通朋友，不是男女朋友。	我们只是普通朋友，不是男女朋友。

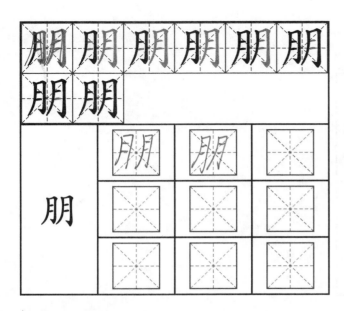

友 (yǒu)

yǒu	Ancient Form	Later Form	Modern Form
friend; friendly; friendship	舛	彐	友
yǒurén			友人

Graphically, 友 is two people's right hands together, signifying 'to give a hand; to help,' which is what friends do for each other. 又 (yòu) also serves as a phonetic component. 朋 and 友 both mean 'friend.' However, 朋 has the connotation of 'to collude,' whereas 友 doesn't. Note that 友 in the word 朋友 is neutral tone. 友 often appears in compound words relating to 'friend,' 'friendship,' or 'befriend.' For example:

友好 friend + good = 'friendly'	友人 friend + person = 'a friend'
校友 school + friend = 'alumni'	男友/女友 man or woman + friend = 'boyfriend; girlfriend'

你的女朋友很有靈氣。	你的女朋友很有灵气。
她的男朋友很帥，也很友好，很客氣。	她的男朋友很帅，也很友好，很客气。
我和那位英俊的藝術家是校友。	我和那位英俊的艺术家是校友。
我的狗很友好，很喜歡和人做朋友。	我的狗很友好，很喜欢和人做朋友。

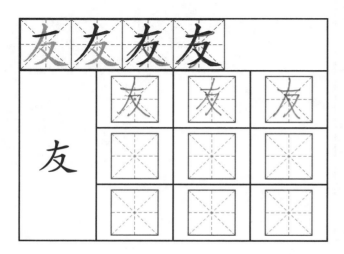

ài	Later Form	Modern Traditional Form	Modern Simplified Form
love; affection; to love; be fond of; be apt to	㤅	愛	爱
àihào		愛好	爱好

The later form of 愛/爱 has a graphic of a heart in the middle as a radical. The top part indicates the pronunciation. The modern form has changed a lot from the later form. In the modern form, there is no part indicating pronunication. The top parts, ⺥ ('hand') and 冖 ('cover'), are combined with the middle part 心 ('heart'), to indicate 'giving heart to others to show love.' In the modern simplified form, the bottom part is changed into 友 ('two right hands together') to indicate friendship.

The primary meaning of 愛/爱 is 'love; to love; affection.' Its meaning is also extended to 'showing passion for certain things or activities.' Therefore, 爱 often appears in compound words relating to 'love,' 'be fond of,' or 'be apt to.' For example:

可愛/可爱 may + love = 'cute; lovely'	愛好/爱好 love + good (pronounced *hào* here) = 'hobby; interests'
母愛/母爱 mother + love = 'motherhood'	愛國/爱国 love + nation = 'patriotic'

你有什麼業餘愛好？	你有什么业余爱好？
他不愛說話，他愛看書。	他不爱说话，他爱看书。
他愛人說我的小狗很可愛。	他爱人说我的小狗很可爱。
我最愛和朋友一起出去玩兒、唱歌、跳舞、認識新朋友。	我最爱和朋友一起出去玩儿、唱歌、跳舞、认识新朋友。

Modern Traditional Form	Modern Simplified Form
愛 愛 愛 愛 愛 愛	爱 爱 爱 爱 爱 爱
愛 愛 愛 愛 愛 愛	爱 爱 爱 爱
愛	

愛				爱	爱		
					爱		

　　　　Copyright © 2012 by Yale University and China International Publishing Group

發/发 (fā)

fā	Later Form	Modern Traditional Form	Modern Simplified Form
shoot out; start off; occur	㿱	發	发
chūfā		出發	出发

The original meaning of 發/发 was 'shoot an arrow.' From that original meaning, 發/发 acquired its extended meaning of 'start off; occur; sprout; grow.' 弓 ('bow') is the radical. 癶 (*bō*) is no longer a useful indicator of the modern pronunciation *fā*. (From the character 佛, now pronounced *fó*, which was used by the ancient Chinese as the word for 'Buddha,' we know that some ancient '*b*' sounds became modern '*f*' sounds.)

The modern simplified form 发 is derived from the cursive writing of 發. Note that 发 is also the simplified form of 髮 'hair.' The context that 发 is used in will clarify its meaning.

發/发 often appears in compound words relating to 'start; shoot out; suddenly occur.' For example:

出發/出发 out + shoot out = 'set out (on a trip, journey)'	發火/发火 shoot out + fire = 'get angry'
發音/发音 shoot out + sound = 'pronunciation'	發言/发言 shoot out + speech = 'make a speech'

在新年，人們見面的時候會説"恭喜發財"。	在新年，人们见面的时候会说"恭喜发财"。
他不愛説話，還常常發火。	他不爱说话，还常常发火。
這個字的發音是什麼？	这个字的发音是什么？
你什麼時候出發去中國？	你什么时候出发去中国？

Modern Traditional Form	Modern Simplified Form

發

发

財/财 *(cái)*

cái	Later Form	Modern Traditional Form	Modern Simplified Form
wealth	財	財	财
fācái		發財	发财

財/财 is a very straightforward picto-phonetic character. The left part, 貝/贝, is the radical, a drawing of a cowrie shell, which in ancient times was a unit of money. The right part, 才 (*cái*), is the phonetic component. We have learned the following characters with 貝/贝 as a component. Do you remember what they mean?

賺/赚 (Unit 6)	貴/贵 (Unit 9)	買/买 (Unit 9)	賣/卖 (Unit 9)	貨/货 (Unit 10)

財/财 often appears in compound words relating to 'wealth' or 'money.' For example:

財氣/财气 wealth + air = 'luck in making big money'	發財/发财 shoot out; grow + wealth = 'make a fortune'
外財/外财 outside + wealth = 'extra income'	財神/财神 wealth + god = 'the god of wealth'

新年好！恭喜發財！	新年好！恭喜发财！
今年我的財氣很好。	今年我的财气很好。
去年他買賣樂器，發大財了。	去年他买卖乐器，发大财了。
當老師賺不到什麼錢，也發不了財。	当老师赚不到什么钱，也发不了财。

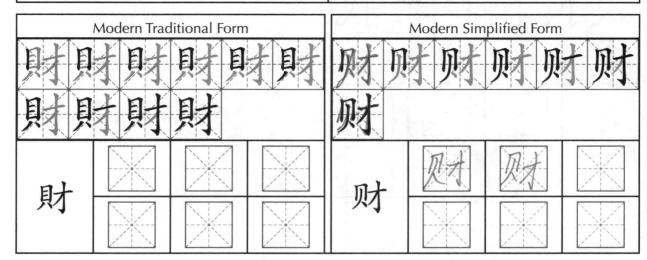

Modern Traditional Form	Modern Simplified Form
財 財 財 財 財 財 財 財 財 財	财 财 财 财 财 财
財	财

Unit 11   17

zhǎo	Later Form	Modern Form
look for; try to find	找	找
zhǎoqián		找錢/找钱

找 is formed with two signific parts. The left part is 手/扌 ('hand') and the right part is 戈 ('dagger-ax,' an ancient weapon). A weapon is usually stowed away when not needed. When it is needed, people need to locate it—to grab it by hand. This was common in the old days. Think of the character this way: in tribal times, a hand that wasn't holding a spear was always 'looking' for one! 找 indicates the action of looking for something. 找 often appears in compound words relating to 'look for.' For example:

找錢/找钱 look for + money = 'give change'	找事 look for + matter = 'look for a job; pick a quarrel'
查找 check + look for = 'look up'	找麻煩/找麻烦 look for + trouble = 'cause someone trouble; ask for trouble'

你在找什麼？找你的書嗎？	你在找什么？找你的书吗？
我的足球找不到了。	我的足球找不到了。
我在等售貨員給我找錢呢。	我在等售货员给我找钱呢。
因為你說他沒出息，他不高興了。你是自己找麻煩。	因为你说他没出息，他不高兴了。你是自己找麻烦。

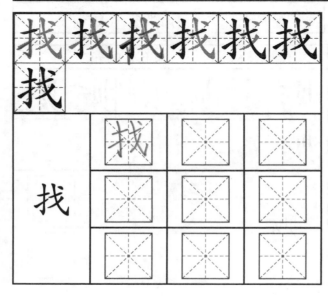

　Copyright © 2012 by Yale University and China International Publishing Group

答 (dá)

dá	Later Form	Modern Form
reply; answer	答	答
huídá		回答

Although there is no clear explanation of the origin of the character 答, here are some clues to help you remember the modern form. 答 has 人 ('person') in the middle and 口 ('mouth') at the bottom, because 答 means 'reply; to answer,' which is done orally. The top part of 答 is the reduced form of 竹 ('bamboo') because one can also reply or answer in writing—and in ancient times, people wrote on bamboo slips. 答 appears in a few compound words relating to 'reply' or 'answer.' For example:

回答 back + reply = 'to reply'	答謝/答谢 reply + thank = 'express appreciation' (*for someone's kindness or hospitality*)
問答/问答 ask + reply = 'question and answer'	答案 reply + file; document = 'answer' (*noun*)

我問了他幾個問題，他回答得很客氣。	我问了他几个问题，他回答得很客气。
對不起，對這個問題，我們現在還沒有答案。	对不起，对这个问题，我们现在还没有答案。
你覺得我應該送她什麼來答謝她的幫助？	你觉得我应该送她什么来答谢她的帮助？
唐教授説完以後，給了二十分鐘的問答時間。	唐教授说完以后，给了二十分钟的问答时间。

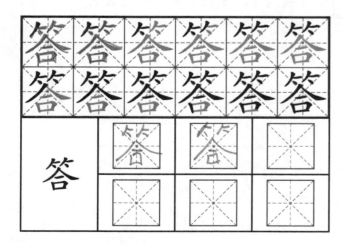

新 (xīn)

xīn	Ancient Form	Later Form	Modern Form
new	𢁅	𣂉	新
xīnnián			新年

The original meaning of the character 新 was 'firewood.' Graphically, the ancient form of 新 is formed with timber on the left and an axe on the right, indicating chopping timber. The later form and modern form both have 斤 (a pictographic character meaning 'ax') on the right, 木 (a pictographic character meaning 'tree; wood') on the bottom left, and 辛 (xīn, a phonetic component) on the top left.

新 meaning 'new' is a phonetic loan. Nowadays, 新 is mostly used to mean 'new.' The original meaning of 'firewood' is now represented by a new character, 薪, which has been created by adding a 艹 ('grass') radical to 新. Think of 新 this way: an ax chopping up some wood to make something 'new.' 新 appears in some compound words relating to 'new; fresh; starting.' For example:

新星 new + star = 'a new star'	新年 new + year = 'new year'
新聞 / 新闻 new + hear = 'news'	清新 clear + new = 'pure and fresh'

他和新認識的女孩子很談得來。	他和新认识的女孩子很谈得来。
我不愛出去跳舞、唱歌，我愛在家看書、聽新聞。	我不爱出去跳舞、唱歌，我爱在家看书、听新闻。
你今天在學校有沒有認識新朋友？	你今天在学校有没有认识新朋友？
新年快到了，咱們去買些新衣服吧。	新年快到了，咱们去买些新衣服吧。

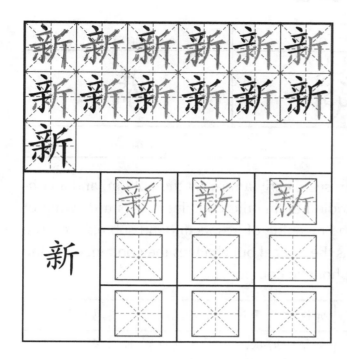

恭 (gōng)

gōng	Later Form	Modern Form
respectful and submissive	萳	恭
gōngxǐ		恭喜

From the later form of this character, you can see clearly a heart at the bottom, and a container at the top, with two hands in the middle holding the container. 恭 is a drawing of worship to a god or a dragon to represent the meaning of 'respectful and submissive.' The modern form keeps the heart at the bottom as the radical but changes the container and the two hands into the character 共 (gòng) as a phonetic component.

聽說你兒子進了很好的大學，恭喜你！	听说你儿子进了很好的大学，恭喜你！
新年的時候，中國人見面的時候會說"新年好，恭喜發財"。	新年的时候，中国人见面的时候会说"新年好，恭喜发财"。
你媽媽說你找到新工作了，恭喜你啊！	你妈妈说你找到新工作了，恭喜你啊！
恭喜你找到了喜歡的工作！	恭喜你找到了喜欢的工作！

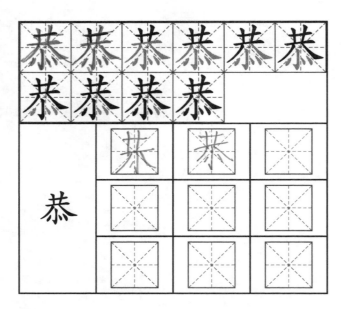

Copyright © 2012 by Yale University and China International Publishing Group

xué	Ancient Form	Later Form	Modern Traditional Form	Modern Simplified Form
study; learn; imitate	𩢆	𦥑	學	学
xuéxiào			學校	学校

The ancient and later forms of 學/学 both have two hands with sticks used for learning counting, and a house. The later form has a 子 ('child') added at the bottom as the radical, since children spend a lot of time learning. 學/学 often appears in compound words relating to 'study,' 'school,' or 'academics.' For example:

學問/学问 study + ask = 'knowledge'	學年/学年 study + year = 'school year'
學期/学期 study + term = 'semester'	大學/大学 big + study = 'university'

這隻鳥會學人説話。	这只鸟会学人说话。
這個學期你要學什麽課?	这个学期你要学什么课?
我想學打毛線。	我想学打毛线。
去年我學了三個星期的中文。	去年我学了三个星期的中文。

Modern Traditional Form	Modern Simplified Form
學 學 學 學 學 學 學 學 學 學 學 學 學 學 學 學	学 学 学 学 学 学 学 学
學	学

老 (lǎo)

lǎo	Ancient Form	Later Form	Modern Form
old; aged; experienced	耂	耆	老
lǎojiā			老家

The ancient form and later form of 老 both look like an old person walking with a crutch. The original meaning of 老 was 'old people.' It has been extended to mean 'old; aged; experienced; tough' (as opposed to 'tender'). 老 often appears in compound words relating to 'old,' 'aged,' or 'experienced.' For example:

老師/老师 old; experienced + master = 'teacher'	老手 old + hand = 'old hand; veteran'
養老/养老 raise + old = 'provide for the aged; live out one's life in retirement'	老家 old + home = 'hometown'

我們的新老師又英俊又聰明。	我们的新老师又英俊又聪明。
我想問老師幾個問題。	我想问老师几个问题。
玩電子遊戲他是老手了。	玩电子游戏他是老手了。
我想請一個老師教我跳舞。	我想请一个老师教我跳舞。

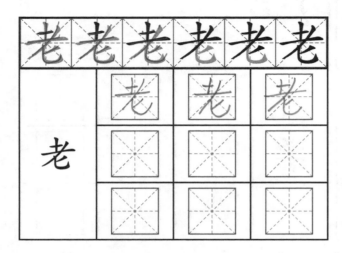

師/师 *(shī)*

shī	Later Form	Modern Traditional Form	Modern Simplified Form
division of army or troops; master; teacher	師	師	师
lǎoshī		老師	老师

The original meaning of 師/师 was 'a division of army.' In modern Chinese this is still one of its most important meanings. From 'division of army,' the meaning of 師/师 was extended to 'military strategist' or 'political strategist.' Later, 師/师 was used to refer to 'anyone who teaches others skills or knowledge.' 師/师 often appears in compound words relating to 'army division,' or 'master.' For example:

師傅/师傅 master + assist = 'a form of address' (*to show respect for skilled professionals*)	師母/师母 master + mother = 'wife of one's teacher or master'
師生/师生 master; teacher + student = 'teacher-student' (*used only before a noun*)	教師/教师 teach + master = 'teacher'

師傅，請送我到火車站。	师傅，请送我到火车站。
你的中文說得越來越好了，你的老師教得很好。	你的中文说得越来越好了，你的老师教得很好。
在我們學校，師生關係非常好。	在我们学校，师生关系非常好。
老師說我的問題問得很好。	老师说我的问题问得很好。

Modern Traditional Form	Modern Simplified Form
師 師 師 師 師 師 師 師 師 師	师 师 师 师 师 师

師				师	师		

寫/写 (*xiě*)

xiě	Later Form	Modern Traditional Form	Modern Simplified Form
write; draw	寫	寫	写
xiězì		寫字	写字

The original meaning of 寫/写 was 'to replace; to relocate.' It has 舄 (*xì*) as the phonetic component and 宀 ('house') as the radical, indicating the whole character is related to space. Remember that writing is something one does under a 'roof.' The traditional phonetic looks a little like the character 兒—just change the 'two legs' of 兒 to the 'tail and four legs' of 舄. The modern simplified form uses the contour of the traditional form.

From 'replace,' the meaning of 寫/写 was extended to 'make a new one by imitating or copying.' In ancient Chinese, 寫/写 meant 'replicate by copying or imitating.' The meaning of 'write' was represented by the character 書/书. Since the Tang Dynasty (618–907 CE), however, 寫/写 has replaced 書/书 in the meaning of 'write.' But in modern Chinese, 書/书 in compound characters sometimes still means 'to write,' such as 書法/书法 ('calligraphy').

寫/写 often appears in compound words relating to 'write' or 'draw.' For example:

書寫/书写 write + write = 'write characters or articles' (*very formal*)	寫法/写法 write + method = 'way of writing characters; calligraphy'
寫生/写生 write + life = 'paint or draw from nature'	寫作/写作 write + make = 'write; compose'

請寫拼音或者漢字。	请写拼音或者汉字。
請用漢字寫一下你的名字。	请用汉字写一下你的名字。
你的中文說得越來越好，你的漢字也寫得越來越好看了。	你的中文说得越来越好，你的汉字也写得越来越好看了。
請你給我寫下來你的電子郵箱，我以後要給你寫信。	请你给我写下来你的电子邮箱，我以后要给你写信。

Modern Traditional Form	Modern Simplified Form
寫 寫 寫 寫 寫 寫	写 写 写 写 写
寫 寫 寫 寫 寫 寫	
寫 寫 寫	

寫					写			

Unit 12

The sentences below are inspired by the contents of Unit 12 and contain all the new characters required for writing as well as others. Read and reread until fluent, covering the English as you read. Then cover the English and try to reproduce the Chinese equivalents orally. Do this exercise before beginning to practice writing.

我喜歡這家超市，因為他們的東西又新鮮 　　又便宜。 我喜欢这家超市，因为他们的东西又新鲜 　　又便宜。	I like this supermarket because their stuff is both fresh and inexpensive.
綠色的蔬菜營養豐富，你應該多吃。 绿色的蔬菜营养丰富，你应该多吃。	Green vegetables are highly nutritious; you should eat more of them.
中國人請客吃飯，總會有雞鴨魚肉。 中国人请客吃饭，总会有鸡鸭鱼肉。	When Chinese people invite guests to a meal, there will always be chicken, duck, fish, and meat.
這些香蕉又香又甜，很好吃。 这些香蕉又香又甜，很好吃。	These bananas are fragrant and sweet; they're delicious.
西瓜和桃子是我最喜歡的水果。 西瓜和桃子是我最喜欢的水果。	Watermelons and peaches are my favorite fruits.
人生跟中國菜一樣，酸甜苦辣都有。 人生跟中国菜一样，酸甜苦辣都有。	Life is like Chinese food—it's sour, sweet, bitter, and spicy.
她不吃豬肉和牛肉，只吃雞肉和海鮮。 她不吃猪肉和牛肉，只吃鸡肉和海鲜。	She doesn't eat pork or beef; she only eats chicken and seafood.
我媽媽做菜很講究，色香味都要好。 我妈妈做菜很讲究，色香味都要好。	My mother is very particular about her cooking; the color, aroma, and taste of the food all have to be good.

What? No Characters? Everything Written in Pinyin?

By now, you need no convincing that learning Chinese characters is hard, much more of a challenge than that posed by alphabetic scripts, such as English. Well, the Chinese have known this for a long, long time. And they have tried, at least since the tail end of the nineteenth century and into the first decades of the twentieth century, to do something about it. Back then, the Chinese noticed that other Asian cultures, by which Chinese characters had been adopted as the way to write their languages, had to varying degrees abandoned the characters in favor of phonetic solutions. Their concerns about the characters were the same as the Chinese: learning the characters is too hard. Therefore, make the language easier to learn; spread literacy, revitalize the country, save it from extinction, and bring the nation into the modern world. The Japanese, for example, developed a syllabary, based on Chinese characters, to write their language, eventually winding up with an amalgam that combined a strictly limited number of borrowed Chinese characters (some of which were changed slightly) with the invented syllabary. A sentence in modern Japanese, after Japan's language reform, looks like this:

'I met Mr. Zhang at the library yesterday'
私は昨日図書館で張氏に会った。

However, even before the Chinese appreciated these reform efforts by other nations, Western missionaries in China, anxious to spread Christianity, had created a phonetic, *pinyin*-like, alphabetic system to transcribe Chinese characters. Native Chinese who worked with the missionaries learned quickly from the missionaries and soon came up with more phonetic representations of the written characters (one of which, created in the middle of the twentieth century, you know already: the *pinyin* variety). Others were created and debated by some of the greatest minds in the nation. Some of the issues included:

1. Should the alphabetized script be derived from Chinese characters (like the Japanese variety) or be based on the Latin letters?
2. Should the alphabetized script be merely a learning-adjunct to the characters, primarily to indicate pronunciation?
3. Should the alphabetized script replace the characters entirely?
4. Should there be one standard language represented by the new script (such as Mandarin), or should the new script represent the major dialects (Cantonese, etc.) as well?
5. Should the new script represent modern spoken Chinese or the classical (文言 [*wényán*]) or some new hybrid?
6. Should the tones be represented in the new script, and if they were, how were they to be indicated? By a superscript (fen^1, fen^2, fen^3, fen^4), or could we spell out the tones with letters (*fen, fern, feen, fenn*)?

All these issues, and others, were hotly debated at all levels, in and out of government. Mao Zedong, interviewed by Edgar Snow in 1936, told the famous American journalist:

> We believe that Latinization [i.e., alphabetization] is a good instrument in order to overcome illiteracy. Chinese characters are so difficult to learn [that] . . . sooner or later, we believe, we will have to abandon characters altogether if we are to create a new social culture in which the masses fully participate. (From *Red Star Over China*, by Edgar Snow [Grove Press, 1968])

With support coming from many quarters, numerous publications became available in the new Latinized script; a full-fledged orthography was created, independent of characters; and a new form of Chinese was expected, especially after the establishment of the People's Republic of China in 1949.

So what happened? In what John DeFrancis has called Mao's 'Great Leap Backward,' Mao directed the government-sponsored language reform effort to start with simplification of the traditionally used characters, and determined that the campaign to create a new alphabetic system should be abandoned. What motivated this turnabout is still unclear. Perhaps one major reason for the change was the opposition of many people, particularly those *already* literate, to any fundamental change in the traditional language, especially one based on an alien, non-Chinese script. Another decision taken by the government was to promote what eventually was called Putonghua (standard Mandarin) as the exclusive standard to be taught nationwide. It appears that the Chinese expected that a simplified script, that is, one that reduced the number of strokes needed to write a character, would serve as a truly mass medium of communication and encourage mass literacy.

Did that happen? Well, literacy in China has improved greatly since the establishment of the People's Republic. Did simplification make the difference? Would literacy still have improved if the traditional characters had not been altered? Is improved literacy simply the result of the nationwide availability of education? Would *pinyinization* have worked?

What do you think?

For more, read *The Chinese Language, Fact and Fantasy,* by John DeFrancis (University of Hawaii Press, 1984). Fascinating stuff.

果 (guǒ)

guǒ	Ancient Form	Later Form	Modern Form
fruit; result			果
Qǐng chī shuǐguǒ.			請吃水果。/ 请吃水果。

果 is a pictographic character meaning 'fruit.' It is also extended to mean 'result.' The ancient form is a sketch of a tree bearing fruit. The later form changes a little bit. It looks like a fruit among leaves on the tree. The modern form keeps 木 (*mù*, 'tree') at the bottom and changes the part at the top of the tree from fruit into 田 (*tián*, 'farmland'). 果 often appears in compound words relating to 'fruit' or 'result':

水果 water + fruit = 'fruit'	蘋果/苹果 apple tree + fruit = 'apple'
後果/后果 after + fruit = 'consequence'	果汁 fruit + extract; juice = 'fruit juice'

今天我家裡請客，我要買很多水果和果汁。	今天我家里请客，我要买很多水果和果汁。
你為什麼讓你的寵物狗喝蘋果汁？	你为什么让你的宠物狗喝苹果汁？
你真的要這樣做嗎？你要想一想這樣做的後果。	你真的要这样做吗？你要想一想这样做的后果。
你最喜歡吃的水果是芒果嗎？	你最喜欢吃的水果是芒果吗？

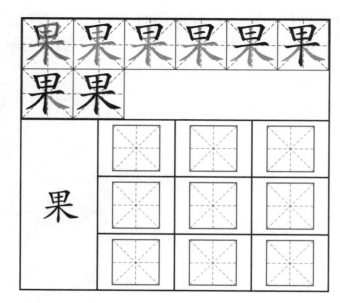

菜 (cài)

cài	Later Form	Modern Form
vegetables; greens; a dish; a course	釆	菜
Zhōngguó cài hěn hǎochī.		中國菜很好吃。/ 中国菜很好吃。

菜 is a picto-phonetic character. The top is the radical 艸 (*cǎo*) (modern form 艹), meaning 'grass.' The bottom part is another radical and the phonetic component 采 (*cǎi*), an associative character (a hand above a tree) meaning 'pick from a plant.' 菜 originally meant only 'vegetables.' In modern Chinese, 菜 is extended to include nonvegetable ingredients one buys from a market. It also refers to a dish or a course. 菜 often appears in compound words relating to 'vegetables,' 'a dish or course,' or 'food.' For example:

菜市 vegetable + market = 'food market'	白菜 white + vegetable = 'cabbage'
菜刀 vegetable + knife = 'kitchen knife'	菜色 vegetable + color = 'sallow and emaciated look'; 'unhealthy look'

我們請客的時候，總是做很多好吃的菜。	我们请客的时候，总是做很多好吃的菜。
你喜歡哪個國家的菜？	你喜欢哪个国家的菜？
這個菜市場的菜很豐富，有很多綠色的蔬菜。	这个菜市场的菜很丰富，有很多绿色的蔬菜。
中國菜又營養，又好吃，越來越多的外國人喜歡吃中國菜了。	中国菜又营养，又好吃，越来越多的外国人喜欢吃中国菜了。

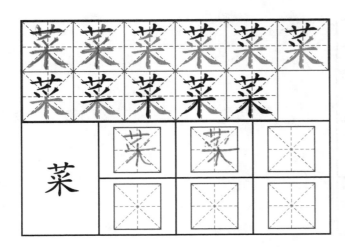

香 (*xiāng*)

xiāng	Ancient Form	Later Form	Modern Form
fragrant; tasty			香
Xiāngjiāo hěn xiāng.			香蕉很香。

The original meaning of 香 was 'the aroma of cereal and grain.' Later it was extended to refer to any good smell or taste. The ancient form of 香 is 禾 (*hé*, 'standing grain,' a pictographic character) on top of 甘 (*gān*). 甘 looks like a sketch of a mouth with something inside, meaning 'delicious' or 'sweet.' The modern form is made up of 禾 and 日, indicating grains sending out an aroma because of the sun. 香 often appears in compound words relating to 'good smell' or 'good taste.' For example:

香水 fragrant + water = 'perfume'	香火 fragrant + fire = 'joss sticks and candles burning at a temple'
香氣/香气 fragrant + air = 'fragrance; aroma'	香菇 fragrant + mushroom = 'mushroom'

這是什麼菜？又香又好看。	这是什么菜？又香又好看。
我在菜市場買了香蕉、香菇、香瓜。	我在菜市场买了香蕉、香菇、香瓜。
他吃得那麼香，好像很多天沒有吃東西了。	他吃得那么香，好像很多天没有吃东西了。
你用的是什麼香水？這麼香！	你用的是什么香水？这么香！

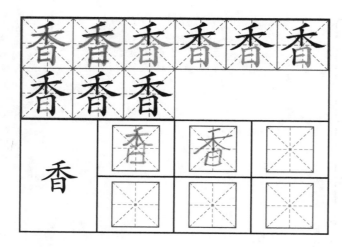

Copyright © 2012 by Yale University and China International Publishing Group

jiāo	Ancient Form	Modern Form
hemp	蕉	蕉
xiāngjiāo		香蕉

蕉 means 'hemp.' It's a picto-phonetic character. The top part, 艸/艹 (*cǎo*, 'grass'), is the radical. The bottom part is the phonetic component 焦 (*jiāo*). 焦 by itself means 'burnt; scorched.' The character is formed with a bird on top of fire. 焦 is a phonetic component in a few compound characters. For example:

木 + 焦 = 樵	忄/心 + 焦 = 憔	目 + 焦 = 瞧	石 + 焦 = 礁
qiáo	*qiáo*	*qiáo*	*jiāo*
firewood	haggard	glance quickly	a reef, rock

你新買的香蕉還不熟，不香。	你新买的香蕉还不熟，不香。
請你給我一根香蕉。	请你给我一根香蕉。
我小時候很少吃香蕉，因為我是在中國的 北方長大的。	我小时候很少吃香蕉，因为我是在中国的 北方长大的。
你為什麼不喜歡吃香蕉？吃香蕉對身體很 好。	你为什么不喜欢吃香蕉？吃香蕉对身体很 好。

guā	Ancient Form	Later Form	Modern Form
melon; gourd	冎	瓜	瓜
xīguā			西瓜

瓜 is a pictographic character. The ancient form is a sketch of a melon hanging from two vines.

瓜 appears in compound words relating to 'melon.' For example:

地瓜 ground; land + melon = 'sweet potato'	香瓜 fragrant + melon = 'cantaloupe'
瓜分 melon + separate = 'divide; carve up'	苦瓜 bitter + melon = 'bitter melon'

你喜歡吃西瓜，還是哈密瓜？	你喜欢吃西瓜，还是哈密瓜？
我不知道為什麼中國人喜歡吃苦瓜。	我不知道为什么中国人喜欢吃苦瓜。
我家旁邊有一個很大的蔬菜瓜果市場。	我家旁边有一个很大的蔬菜瓜果市场。
我最喜歡的水果是西瓜，不是香蕉。	我最喜欢的水果是西瓜，不是香蕉。

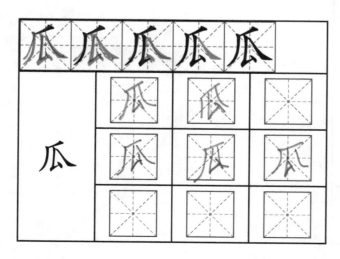

桃 (táo)

táo	Ancient Form	Modern Form
peach	桃	桃
Qǐng chī táozi.		請吃桃子。/ 请吃桃子。

桃 is a picto-phonetic character. 木 (*mù*, 'tree'; 'plant'), on the left, is the radical, indicating that the whole character is related to 'tree.' 兆 (*zhào*), on the right, is the phonetic component.

We have learned a few characters with the 木 radical. Can you recognize the following characters? 菜, 梨, 梳, 杯. Can you list more?

你今天買的桃子又大又甜。	你今天买的桃子又大又甜。
這個水果市場沒有櫻桃，只有桃子和獼猴桃。	这个水果市场没有櫻桃，只有桃子和猕猴桃。
這種桃子雖然不紅，可是又香又甜。	这种桃子虽然不红，可是又香又甜。
市場上有很多不同的桃子，有紅色的桃子，有粉紅色的桃子，還有白色的桃子。	市场上有很多不同的桃子，有红色的桃子，有粉红色的桃子，还有白色的桃子。

桃 桃 桃 桃 桃 桃　　兆
桃 桃 桃 桃

桃

酸 (*suān*)

suān	Ancient Form	Modern Form
sour; acid	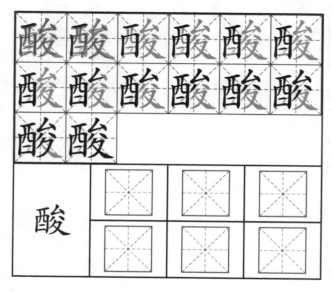 醻	酸
Zhège táozi yǒudiǎn suān.		這個桃子有點酸。 / 这个桃子有点酸。

酸 is a picto-phonetic character. It is the original character for 'vinegar.' The left part, 酉 (*yǒu*, 'vase'), is the radical, indicating that the whole character is related to 'jar' or 'fermentation.' The right part, 夋 (*qūn*), is the phonetic component. Since vinegar smells and tastes sour, gradually 酸 came to mean 'sour.' Later a new character, 醋 (*cù*), was created for 'vinegar.' When one cries, one feels a lump in the throat and twitches in the nose—a reaction similar to that of eating sour food. Therefore, 酸 is also used to describe 'feelings of grief and sadness.' 酸 appears in compound words relating to 'sour,' 'acid,' or 'sadness.' For example:

心酸 heart + sour = 'feel sad'	酸奶 sour + milk = 'yogurt'
酸甜苦辣 sour + sweet + bitter + spicy = 'joys and sorrows of life'	酸菜 sour + vegetable = 'pickled Chinese cabbage'

我不喜歡酸的東西。	我不喜欢酸的东西。
這個桃子雖然很紅，可是很酸。	这个桃子虽然很红，可是很酸。
這種果汁酸酸甜甜的，真好喝。	这种果汁酸酸甜甜的，真好喝。

甜 (tián)

tián	Later Form	Modern Form
sweet; pleasant	甛	甜
tiándiǎn		甜點／甜点

Comparing the later form with the modern form of 甜, you will see that the left part and right part of this character have switched places. This was done for consistency: when 甘 appears in a compound character, it is usually on the right. 甜 means 'sweet.' It has 甘 (*gān*) (the left part of the later form and the right part of the modern form) as the radical. 甘 looks like a mouth with something inside, indicating 'delicious' or 'sweet.' 甜 has 舌 (*shé*, 'tongue') as another radical, indicating that the whole character 甜 is related to tongue. 舌 itself looks like a tongue sticking out of a mouth. Of the five tastes—sour, sweet, bitter, spicy, salty—甜 is the only pleasing taste. Therefore, 甜 has an extended meaning of 'pleasant.' 甜 appears in compound words relating to 'sweet' or 'pleasant.' For example:

甜點／甜点 sweet + little dot = 'dessert; sweet snacks'	甜美 sweet + beautiful = 'sweet; refreshing; pleasant'
酸甜苦辣 sour + sweet + bitter + spicy = 'joys and sorrows of life'	香甜 fragrant + sweet = 'fragrant and sweet'; 'sound' (as in a sound sleep)

美國人喜歡吃完飯以後吃甜點。	美国人喜欢吃完饭以后吃甜点。
你看這個小孩子睡得那麼香甜。	你看这个小孩子睡得那么香甜。
她甜甜地對我笑了笑。	她甜甜地对我笑了笑。

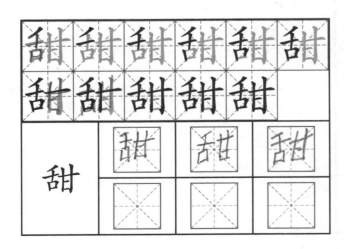

苦 (kǔ)

kǔ	Later Form	Modern Form
bitter; hardship	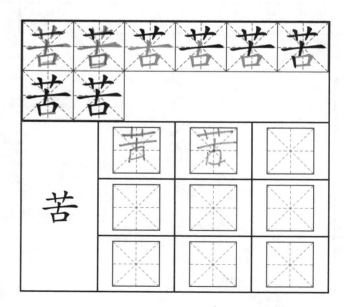	苦
suāntiánkǔlà		酸甜苦辣

苦 is a picto-phonetic character. Its original meaning was 'bitter edible plant.' 艸/艹 ('grass'), at the top, is the radical. 古 (*gǔ*, 'ancient'), at the bottom, is the phonetic component. 苦 in modern Chinese means 'bitter' or 'hardship.' It appears in compound words relating to 'bitter,' 'suffering,' or 'hardship.' For example:

苦工 bitter + work = 'hard labor; toil'	苦瓜 bitter + melon = 'bitter melon'
苦笑 bitter + smile = 'forced smile'	吃苦 eat + bitter = 'bear hardship'

每個人的生活都有酸甜苦辣。	每个人的生活都有酸甜苦辣。
我不知道為什麼中國人喜歡吃苦瓜。	我不知道为什么中国人喜欢吃苦瓜。
中國父母覺得孩子小的時候吃點苦是應該的。	中国父母觉得孩子小的时候吃点苦是应该的。
有的水果不熟的時候，有點苦味或者酸味。	有的水果不熟的时候，有点苦味或者酸味。

Copyright © 2012 by Yale University and China International Publishing Group

là	Later Form	Modern Form
spicy; peppery; ruthless	粹	辣
suāntiánkǔlà		酸甜苦辣

辣 is a picto-phonetic character. In the modern form, the left part and right part have switched places from the later form. 辛 (*xīn*, 'pungent') is the radical. 剌 (*là*) is the original phonetic component, but it is simplified as 束 in 辣. As a result, 束 here is no longer a reliable phonetic component. 辣 appears in a few compound words relating to 'spicy,' 'peppery,' or 'ruthless.' For example:

心狠手辣 heart + hateful + hand + ruthless = 'extremely cruel and merciless'	熱辣辣/热辣辣 hot + spicy = 'scorching'
酸甜苦辣 sour + sweet + bitter + spicy = 'joys and sorrows of life'	火辣辣 fire + spicy = 'burning; scorching'

四川菜都很辣。	四川菜都很辣。
韓國人很能吃辣。	韩国人很能吃辣。
每個人的生活都有酸甜苦辣。	每个人的生活都有酸甜苦辣。
我不能吃辣的菜，別的什麼菜都能吃。	我不能吃辣的菜，别的什么菜都能吃。

牛 (niú)

niú	Ancient Form	Later Form	Modern Form
ox; cow	Ψ	Ψ	牛
niúnǎi			牛奶

牛 is a pictographic character. The ancient form looks like the head of an ox. The long and curved horns are emphasized. In the modern form, the upward-pointing horns became a left-slanting stroke and a horizontal stroke. This transformation might make more sense and be easier to remember if you know that 牛 also means 'cow,' and some cows don't have horns. 牛 often appears in compound words relating to 'cattle.' For example:

牛肉 ox; cow + meat = 'beef'	牛奶 cow + milk = '(cow's) milk'
奶牛 milk + cow = 'milk cow'	水牛 water + ox; cow = 'buffalo'

明天我要在家裡請客，今天我買了水果和牛肉。	明天我要在家里请客，今天我买了水果和牛肉。
家裡的牛奶喝完了，你明天回家的路上要買牛奶。	家里的牛奶喝完了，你明天回家的路上要买牛奶。
我不喜歡喝牛奶，我喜歡吃酸奶。	我不喜欢喝牛奶，我喜欢吃酸奶。
小時候我家裡養了一頭牛。	小时候我家里养了一头牛。

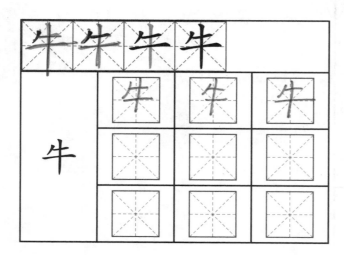

魚/鱼 (*yú*)

yú	Ancient Form	Later Form	Modern Traditional Form	Modern Simplified Form
fish			魚	鱼
yì tiáo dà yú			一條大魚	一条大鱼

魚/鱼, a pictographic character, is a sketch of a fish with head, body, scales, and tail. Note that in both modern forms, the fish body with scales is represented by 田 (tián, 'farmland'), even though that has nothing to do with fish. 魚/鱼 appears in compound words relating to 'fish.' For example:

魚肉/鱼肉 fish + meat = 'fish meat'	魚子/鱼子 fish + child = 'roe'
金魚/金鱼 gold + fish = 'goldfish'	美人魚/美人鱼 beautiful + person + fish = 'mermaid'

你今天買回來的這條魚真新鮮。	你今天买回来的这条鱼真新鲜。
中國人喜歡吃魚頭，美國人都不吃魚頭。	中国人喜欢吃鱼头，美国人都不吃鱼头。
他游泳游得像魚一樣快。	他游泳游得像鱼一样快。
你不要吃太多炸魚。	你不要吃太多炸鱼。

Modern Traditional Form	Modern Simplified Form

鮮/鲜 (*xiān*)

xiān	Later Form	Modern Traditional Form	Modern Simplified Form
fresh; delicious; new	鮮	鮮	鲜
hǎixiān		海鮮	海鲜

It's quite easy to remember the character 鮮/鲜. Put 魚/鱼 (yú, 'fish') and 羊 (yáng, 'sheep,' 'lamb') together, and you have a new character meaning 'fresh and delicious.' 鮮/鲜 originally meant a specific kind of fish. 魚/鱼, on the left, is one radical, indicating that the whole character is related to fish. 羊, on the right, is another radical, indicating that this kind of fish tastes as delicious as the meat of lamb. From the meaning of 'a delicious kind of fish,' 鮮/鲜 got its extended meaning of 'delicious,' 'fresh.' Gradually, its original meaning of 'a kind of fish' was dropped. 鮮/鲜 appears in compound words relating to 'fresh,' 'new,' or 'delicious.' For example:

鮮紅/鲜红 fresh + red = 'bright red'	鮮亮/鲜亮 fresh + bright = 'brilliant; well defined' (*colors, images*)
鮮花/鲜花 fresh + flower = 'fresh flower'	鮮果/鲜果 fresh + fruit = 'fresh fruit'

你喜歡吃海鮮嗎？	你喜欢吃海鲜吗？
那件衣服的顏色很鮮亮。	那件衣服的颜色很鲜亮。
昨天我男朋友送給我一把鮮花。	昨天我男朋友送给我一把鲜花。

Modern Traditional Form	Modern Simplified Form
鮮 鮮 鮮 鮮 鮮 鮮 鮮 鮮 鮮 鮮 鮮 鮮 鮮 鮮 鮮 鮮 鮮	鲜 鲜 鲜 鲜 鲜 鲜 鲜 鲜 鲜 鲜 鲜 鲜

味 (wèi)

wèi	Later Form	Modern Form
taste; smell	𣘤	味
kǒuwèi		口味

味 is a picto-phonetic character. 口 (kǒu, 'mouth'), on the left, is the radical, indicating that the whole character is related to 'mouth.' 未 (wèi), on the right, is the phonetic component. 味 means 'taste.' Since the senses of mouth and nose are interlinked, 味 is also used to mean 'smell.' Later, 味 was extended to mean 'the taste, feeling, and interest of the heart.' 味 appears in compound words relating to 'taste,' 'smell,' or 'interest.' For example:

意味 thought + taste = 'meaning; implication'	氣味 / 气味 air + taste = 'smell'
回味 back + taste = 'aftertaste'; 'call to mind and ponder'	口味 mouth + taste = 'one's taste'

中國北方人和南方人的口味不太一樣。	中国北方人和南方人的口味不太一样。
我吃菜的口味很淡，所以這個菜太鹹了。	我吃菜的口味很淡，所以这个菜太咸了。
房子裡有很清香的氣味。	房子里有很清香的气味。
他對我說的話讓我回味了很長時間。	他对我说的话让我回味了很长时间。

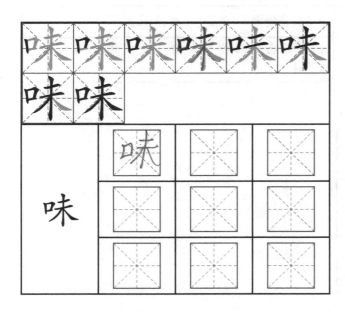

肉 (ròu)

ròu	Ancient Form	Later Form	Modern Form
meat; flesh	刀	⟨later form⟩	肉
niúròu			牛肉

肉 is a pictographic character. The ancient form of 肉 is a sketch of a piece of meat with ribs. Note that when 肉 is a component of a compound character, it appears as 月, the character's later form. For example: 肝 (*gān*, 'liver'), 肚 (*dù*, 'belly'), and 背 (*bèi*, 'back'). For that reason, when you see 月 in a compound character, you need to decide whether it means 'moon' or 'meat; body part.' Can you guess what 月 means in each of the following characters? Does the meaning of the entire character help? Consult a dictionary to find out the answers.

肥 'fat'	朗 'bright; clear'	胭 'rouge; makeup'	胃 'stomach'	朝 'morning'	肖 'similar; likeness'

肉 appears in compound words relating to 'meat' or 'flesh.' For example:

肉店 meat + store = 'butcher's (shop)'	豬肉/猪肉 pig + meat = 'pork'
牛肉 ox; cow + meat = 'beef'	果肉 fruit + meat; flesh = 'flesh of fruit; pulp of fruit'

我丈夫每天都要吃肉，只有蔬菜不行。	我丈夫每天都要吃肉，只有蔬菜不行。
雖然他喜歡吃肉，但他口味很淡。	虽然他喜欢吃肉，但他口味很淡。
牛肉、豬肉、羊肉，都是紅肉。	牛肉、猪肉、羊肉，都是红肉。
這個飯店的海鮮很新鮮，魚肉做得非常好吃。	这个饭店的海鲜很新鲜，鱼肉做得非常好吃。

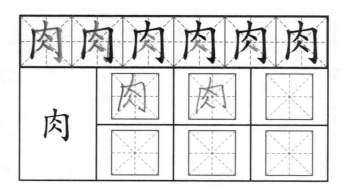

zhū	Later Form	Modern Traditional Form	Modern Simplified Form
swine; pig	豬	豬	猪
zhūròu		豬肉	猪肉

豬/猪 is a picto-phonetic character. 者 (*zhě*), on the right, is the phonetic component. The left part of the later form is the radical 豕 (*shǐ*, 'pig'). You've already learned 豕 in the character 家 (*jiā*, 'home'). (Since the pig was the first domestic animal, a building with a pig signifies the dwelling place of a human being.) In the modern simplified form, 豕 becomes 犭.

豬肉怎麼做都好吃。	猪肉怎么做都好吃。
我喜歡吃豬肉韭菜包子。	我喜欢吃猪肉韭菜包子。
德國人每年吃的豬肉最多。	德国人每年吃的猪肉最多。
牛肉、羊肉、豬肉，你喜歡吃哪個？	牛肉、羊肉、猪肉，你喜欢吃哪个？

Modern Traditional Form	Modern Simplified Form
豬 豬 豬 豬 豬 豬	猪 猪 猪 猪 猪 猪
豬 豬 豬 豬 豬 豬	猪 猪 猪 猪 猪
豬 豬 豬	
豬	猪

雞/鸡 (jī)

jī	Ancient Form	Later Form	Modern Traditional Form	Modern Simplified Form
chicken	𩾌	雞	雞	鸡
jīdàn			雞蛋	鸡蛋

The ancient form of 雞/鸡 is a sketch of a chicken, and it is a pictographic character. In the later form and modern traditional form, 隹 (*zhuī*, a radical indicating 'bird'), on the right, is used as the radical. 奚 (*xī*), on the left, is the phonetic component. The modern simplified form uses 鸟 (*niǎo*, meaning 'small bird') instead of 隹 as the radical and replaces 奚 with 又 to simplify the character. 又 is not a signific or phonetic component here; however, you should know that 又 by itself means 'right hand.' When 又 is used in a compound character, it usually indicates that the whole character is related to 'hand action.' For the simplifed form of 鸡, you can associate the meaning 'chicken' with 'a bird you can catch with your hands.' 雞/鸡 appears in compound words relating to 'chicken.' For example:

母雞/母鸡 female + chicken = 'hen'	公雞/公鸡 male + chicken = 'rooster; cock'
火雞/火鸡 fire (*think about the turkey's tail*) + chicken = 'turkey'	炸雞/炸鸡 fry + chicken = 'fried chicken'

雞鴨魚肉，你喜歡吃什麼？	鸡鸭鱼肉，你喜欢吃什么？
美國人每年都吃很多火雞。	美国人每年都吃很多火鸡。
我每天都要吃兩個雞蛋。	我每天都要吃两个鸡蛋。
吃太多炸雞對身體不好。	吃太多炸鸡对身体不好。

Modern Traditional Form	Modern Simplified Form
雞 雞 雞 雞 雞 雞 雞 雞 雞 雞 雞 雞 雞 雞 雞 雞 雞 雞	鸡 鸡 鸡 鸡 鸡 鸡 鸡
雞	鸡

chāo	Later Form	Modern Form
leap over; exceed; superb	超	超
chāoshì		超市

The original meaning of 超 was 'jump over' or 'pass.' It is a picto-phonetic character. 走 (*zǒu*, 'walk'), on the left, is the radical, indicating that the whole character is related to 'foot.' 召 (*zhào*), on the right, is the phonetic component. Later 超 was extended to mean 'exceed' and 'superb.' 超 appears in compound words relating to 'exceed' or 'superb.' For example:

超市 superb + market = 'supermarket'	超常 exceed + common = 'extraordinary'
高超 high; tall + exceed = 'superb; excellent'	超期 exceed + term = 'overdue'

以前中國沒有超市，現在超市越來越多了。	以前中国没有超市，现在超市越来越多了。
他有非常高超的做飯技巧。	他有非常高超的做饭技巧。
這個超市只賣雞鴨魚肉，沒有什麼水果。	这个超市只卖鸡鸭鱼肉，没有什么水果。
這個孩子對音樂有超常的天分(*tiānfèn*, 'natural talent')。	这个孩子对音乐有超常的天分 (*tiānfèn*, 'natural talent')。

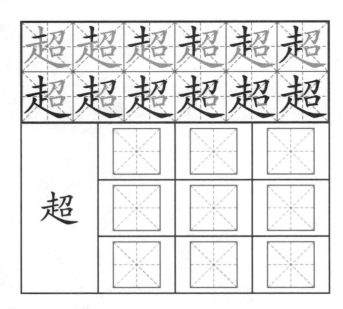

Copyright © 2012 by Yale University and China International Publishing Group

市 (shì)

shì	Later Form	Modern Form
market; city	业	市
shìchǎng		市場 / 市场

The later form of 市 has 止 (zhǐ, 'foot') on the top, indicating 'going to a place.' The bottom part is 兮 (xī), indicating a place full of noise, which is one characteristic of a marketplace. As for the modern form, use your own imagination. 市 is a place with a 冂 ('wall') and a sign (the dot on the top). 市 appears in compound words relating to 'market' or 'city.' For example:

花市 flower + market = 'flower market'	早市 early + market = 'morning market'
市场 market + field = 'market'	城市 wall + city = 'city'

城市裡的人多，車也多。	城市里的人多，车也多。
我喜歡去早市，空氣新鮮，東西也便宜。	我喜欢去早市，空气新鲜，东西也便宜。
現在美國的房子市場非常不好。	现在美国的房子市场非常不好。
這個超市是新開的，東西又好又便宜。	这个超市是新开的，东西又好又便宜。

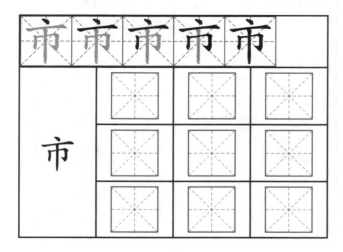

綠/绿 (lǜ)

lǜ	Ancient Form	Modern Traditional Form	Modern Simplified Form
green	綠	綠	绿
lǜsè		綠色	绿色

綠/绿 is a picto-phonetic character. 糸 / 纟 (which sometimes appears as 糸), on the left, is the radical, which indicates that this character is related to 'silk' or 'cloth.' 录 (lù), on the right, is the phonetic component. We have learned quite a few characters that have 糸 / 纟 or 糸 as a radical. Recall the following characters: 級/级 (jí, 'level; rank; grade'); 紅/红 (hóng, 'red'); 給/给 (gěi).

這兒的海水真綠。	这儿的海水真绿。
你不要吃那麼多炸雞，你應該多吃綠色的蔬菜。	你不要吃那么多炸鸡，你应该多吃绿色的蔬菜。
我不喜歡吃綠菜花，我喜歡吃白菜花。	我不喜欢吃绿菜花，我喜欢吃白菜花。
我覺得中國的綠色蔬菜比美國的多。	我觉得中国的绿色蔬菜比美国的多。

Modern Traditional Form	Modern Simplified Form
綠 綠 綠 綠 綠 綠 綠 綠 綠 綠 綠 綠 綠 綠	绿 绿 绿 绿 绿 绿 绿 绿 绿
綠	绿

sè	Later Form	Modern Form
color; look	㠯	色
yánsè		顏色/颜色

The later form of 色 is like a person on top of another person. The original meaning of 色 was 'making love.' Later it was extended to mean 'beautiful female appearance.' Gradually, 色 came to represent 'facial expression,' 'appearance,' and 'color.' 色 appears in compound words relating to 'color,' 'look,' or 'sex.' For example:

天色 sky + color = 'time of day as shown by the color of the sky'	色情 sex + feelings = 'pornographic'
肉色 flesh + color = 'flesh color; yellow-ish pink'	菜色 vegetable + color = 'sallow and emaciated look; unhealthy look'

他做的菜色香味都好。	他做的菜色香味都好。
你喜歡什麼顏色?	你喜欢什么颜色?
這種綠色的蔬菜叫什麼名字?	这种绿色的蔬菜叫什么名字?
天色不早了，我該走了。	天色不早了，我该走了。

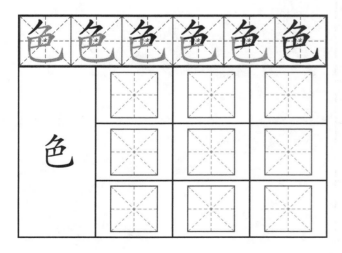

shū	Later Form	Modern Form
vegetables; greens	𦼪	蔬
shūcài		蔬菜

蔬 is a picto-phonetic character. 艸/艹 (*cǎo*, 'plant'; 'grass'), on the top, is the radical, indicating that the whole character is related to 'plant' or 'grass.' 疏 (*shū*), at the bottom, is the phonetic component. You will see 疏 in the future. We have learned a few characters with the 艸/艹 radical. Can you recognize the following characters—菜, 苦, 花, 英? Can you list more?

你去早市上買些蔬菜水果吧。	你去早市上买些蔬菜水果吧。
他不吃肉，只吃蔬菜和雞蛋。	他不吃肉，只吃蔬菜和鸡蛋。
現在蔬菜比肉貴。	现在蔬菜比肉贵。
你也要多吃綠色的蔬菜。	你也要多吃绿色的蔬菜。

Copyright © 2012 by Yale University and China International Publishing Group

Unit 13

The sentences below are inspired by the contents of Unit 13 and contain all the new characters required for writing as well as others. Read and reread until fluent, covering the English as you read. Then cover the English and try to reproduce the Chinese equivalents orally. Do this exercise before beginning to practice writing.

到別人家裡作客，帶個禮物，主人會很高興。 到别人家里作客，带个礼物，主人会很高兴。	When you're a guest in someone else's home, bring a gift; the host will be pleased.
你明天有空嗎？我想請你喝咖啡。 你明天有空吗？我想请你喝咖啡。	Are you free tomorrow? I'd like to invite you out for coffee.
這個問題真簡單。 这个问题真简单。	This question is really simple.
這只是一點心意，希望你會喜歡。 这只是一点心意，希望你会喜欢。	This is just a small expression of my regards; I hope you'll like it.
她很客氣地説：別太麻煩，甚麼都行。 她很客气地说：别太麻烦，什么都行。	She said politely, 'Don't go to too much trouble; anything would be fine.'
我想送我爸爸一個生日禮物。 我想送我爸爸一个生日礼物。	I'd like to give my father a birthday present.
我愛喝茶，不喜歡喝咖啡。 我爱喝茶，不喜欢喝咖啡。	I love drinking tea; I don't like drinking coffee.
要是你想請我吃飯，我當然想去。 要是你想请我吃饭，我当然想去。	If you want to invite me to a meal, I of course would like to go.

How to Locate the Radical in a Chinese Character: The Seven Questions

You will soon be regularly using a Chinese character dictionary in order to make further progress in reading Chinese. In order to quickly and reliably use a Chinese dictionary, you need to be able to rapidly locate *where* the radical is in the character. Remember that recognizing the radical gives you a clue to the character's meaning. Thus radical identification is doubly helpful, since successful identification both gives a clue to meaning and helps in navigating a Chinese dictionary.

To reliably identify the radical of any character, ask the 'Seven Questions' and stop at the first question that can be answered in the affirmative. An affirmative answer will almost always mean that you have found the radical, the first step when using a Chinese dictionary to find a character for which you do not know the meaning or pronunciation.

Question 1. *Top?* Is there a clear top radical?

    Examples: 家 (宀); 早 (日); 男 (田); 爸 (父)

Question 2. *Bottom?* Is there a clear bottom radical?

    Examples: 想 (心); 貴/贵 (貝/贝); 熱/热 (灬)

Question 3. *Left?* Is there a clearly defined left radical? 'Clearly defined' means that the left-side radical completely dominates the left side and is unobstructed both above and below. Note that the radical may touch the right side but may not intrude into it. MOST of the radicals in the language are on the LEFT side.

    Examples: 和 (禾); 他 (亻); 吗/嗎 (口); 明 (日); 打 (扌)

Question 4. *Right?* Is there a clearly defined right radical that may touch but may not intrude into the character? The right is another favorite place for the radical to 'hang out.'

    Examples: 別 (刂); 對/对 (寸); 期 (月)

Question 5. *Enclosure?* Does the character have a completely exterior enclosure radical? The test is whether the radical actually encloses two or more sides. Examples:

    Two sides: 病 (疒); 店 (广); 遠/远 (辶)
    Three sides: 同 (冂); 問/问 (門/门)
    Four sides: 四 (囗); 圓/园 (囗); 回 (囗); 國/国 (囗)

After these five questions, which will identify most radicals, then ask:

Question 6. *All?* Is the entire character a radical? Many characters with very few strokes are of this variety.

    Examples: 方   生   大   口   木   水   火

Question 7. *Lone?* Does the character have only one lone radical that is often not clearly defined? There are very few such characters in common use. Here are a few:

Examples: 了 (一); 及 (又); 久 (丿); 九 (丿)

These 'Seven Questions' will determine the location of the radical for about 97% of all characters—not a bad first step in what is admittedly a difficult task. But, you may ask, what about the remaining 3%? For those few characters, the answer may lie in one of the *corners*, so start in the corners, working clockwise from the northwest. Here are some examples:

northwest: 報 (土)

northeast: 长 (丿) (长 is the simplified form; the traditional form, 長, is a radical in itself!*)

southeast: 君 (口)

southwest: 虱 (虫)

Exercise: ask the 'Seven Questions' and see if you can locate the radicals of the ten characters below. Work with your classmates; share opinions and findings. Write your guess at the proper radical below each character.

The Seven Questions: Top? Bottom? Left? Right? Enclosure? All? Lone?

浪	葡	梨	一	衣	音	基	因	劫	匹

(*answers on last page of this unit*)

---

*This leads us to yet another caution: the simplification process has led to further complications, such as the elimination of some radicals (like 長). It all seems very complicated, and it is, but practice will make the whole process easier to manage.

主 (*zhǔ*)

zhǔ	Later Form	Modern Form
chief; primary; main	![lamp wick]	主
zhǔrén		主人

Can you see a lamp wick with a lamp holder in the later form of 主? 主 is a pictographic character. The original meaning of 主 was 'lamp wick.' Since the lamp wick is the center of a lamp, 主 is extended to mean 'main,' 'primary,' 'chief.' 主 is also used in a compound verb meaning 'be in charge of,' 'direct.' The meaning 'lamp wick' is now represented by a new character, 炷, which was created by adding the 火 ('fire') radical to 主. Think of 主 this way: in the old days, when you knocked on someone's door at night, the host would open the door holding an oil lamp. 主 often appears in compound words relating to 'main,' 'primary,' or 'be in charge of.' For example:

主人 main + person = 'host'	主見/主见 main + view = 'one's own ideas'
主食 main + eat = 'staple foods' (cereals, rice, buns, etc.)	主客 main + guest = 'guest of honor'

對這件事我一點主意都沒有，你幫我出個主意吧。	对这件事我一点主意都没有，你帮我出个主意吧。
你不能只吃菜，你得吃點主食。	你不能只吃菜，你得吃点主食。
他是一個很有主見的孩子。	他是一个很有主见的孩子。
明天我們家要請客，主客是爸爸的老朋友。	明天我们家要请客，主客是爸爸的老朋友。

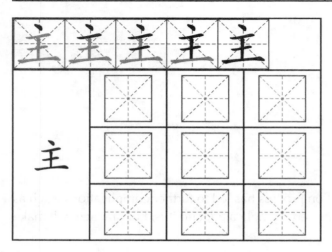

空 (kòng)

kòng	Ancient Form	Later Form	Modern Form
spare time; blank space; vacant			空
Wǒ jīntiān méi kòng.			我今天没空。

The original meaning of 空 was 'hole' and 'cave.' Doesn't the ancient form of 空 look like a cave? From 'hole' and 'cave,' 空 was extended to mean 'not occupied,' in terms of both space and time. 穴 (*xué*, 'cave') is the radical. 工 (*gōng*) is the phonetic component. 空 appears in a few compound words relating to 'spare time,' 'free time,' or 'empty space.' For example:

空白 empty space + white = 'blank space' (on a page or book)	空地 empty space + ground; land = 'open ground; vacant lot'

Note that 空, when pronounced *kōng*, is also used to mean 'empty' and 'hollow,' as in the following compound words:

天空 sky + empty = 'sky'	空談/空谈 empty + talk = 'prattle'

你今天有空(*kòng*)嗎？我想請你幫個忙。	你今天有空(*kòng*)吗？我想请你帮个忙。
這一片空(*kòng*)地空(*kòng*)了很長時間了。	这一片空(*kòng*)地空(*kòng*)了很长时间了。
不要總是空(*kōng*)談你長大以後要做什麼，現在要好好學習。	不要总是空(*kōng*)谈你长大以后要做什么，现在要好好学习。
現在天空(*kōng*)中的星星越來越少了。	现在天空(*kōng*)中的星星越来越少了。

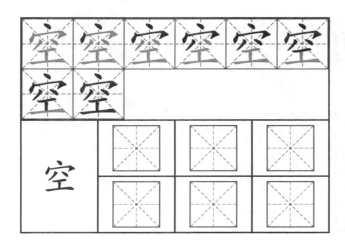

喝 (*hē*)

hē	Later Form	Modern Form
drink	喝	喝
Nǐ xiǎng hē diǎn shénme?		你想喝點甚麼? / 你想喝点什么?

喝 is a picto-phonetic character. 口 ('mouth'), on the left, is the radical, indicating that the whole character is related to 'mouth.' 曷 (*hé*), on the right, is the phonetic component. 喝 was originally pronounced as *hè*, meaning 'shout,' 'call out.' The meaning 'to drink' was represented by the character 飲/饮 (*yǐn*). In modern Chinese, 飲/饮 appears in compound words meaning 'something to drink' (as in 飲料/饮料), while 喝 acquires a different proununciaton (*hē*) and stands alone to mean 'to drink.' 'Shout; call out' is still the primary meaning of 喝 (*hè*) when it appears in compound words such as 喝彩/喝采 ('cheer; acclaim').

你現在有空嗎? 我想請你喝咖啡。	你现在有空吗? 我想请你喝咖啡。
這幾天沒事做, 每天就是吃吃喝喝的。	这几天没事做, 每天就是吃吃喝喝的。
你喜歡喝茶還是喝咖啡?	你喜欢喝茶还是喝咖啡?
我喜歡喝口味淡的東西。	我喜欢喝口味淡的东西。

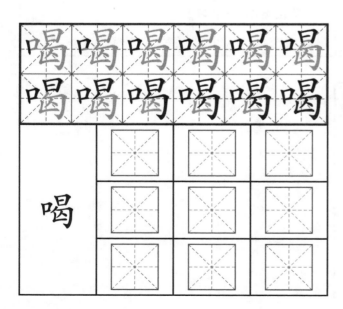

chá	Later Form	Modern Form
tea	茶	茶
Wǒ ài hē chá.		我愛喝茶。/ 我爱喝茶。

茶 is a picto-phonetic character. 艸/艹 ('grass,' 'plant') at the top is the radical. The bottom part used to be the phonetic component but isn't any more. You can view the bottom part as 木 ('tree'), a tea plant. 茶 appears in some compound words relating to 'tea.' For example:

紅茶/红茶 red + tea = 'black tea'	綠茶/绿茶 green + tea = 'green tea'
花茶 flower + tea = 'scented tea'	茶館/茶馆 tea + accommodation for guests = 'teahouse'

中國人喜歡喝茶，美國人喜歡喝咖啡。	中国人喜欢喝茶，美国人喜欢喝咖啡。
現在中國的茶館不太多了。	现在中国的茶馆不太多了。
你喜歡喝紅茶、綠茶還是花茶？	你喜欢喝红茶、绿茶还是花茶？
天氣這麼熱，你怎麼還喝熱茶？	天气这么热，你怎么还喝热茶？

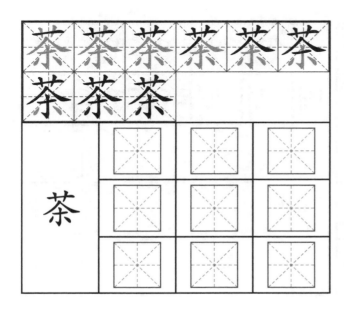

kā	Modern Form
(a character used in transliterating)	咖

fēi	Modern Form
(a character used in transliterating)	啡
kāfēi	咖啡

Both 咖 and 啡 are newly created characters for transliterating. 咖 is also used in 咖喱 (*gālí*, 'curry'). Both characters have 口 ('mouth') as the radical, indicating that the character is related to 'mouth,' and, by extension, to a transliterated word. 加 (*jiā*) and 非 (*fēi*), on the right sides of the characters, are the phonetic components.

我覺得咖啡有苦味，我不喜歡喝咖啡。	我觉得咖啡有苦味，我不喜欢喝咖啡。
美國人每天早上都要喝咖啡。	美国人每天早上都要喝咖啡。
你喝咖啡喜歡加牛奶嗎？	你喝咖啡喜欢加牛奶吗？
你喜歡喝咖啡還是喝茶？	你喜欢喝咖啡还是喝茶？

咖 咖 咖 咖 咖 咖 咖 咖

啡 啡 啡 啡 啡 啡 啡 啡 啡 啡 啡

咖

啡

xī	Later Form	Modern Form
hope; expect	爷	希
xīwàng		希望

希 is formed with 巾 (*jīn*), which means 'cloth,' and 爻 (*yáo*), which looks like a stitch. The original meaning of 希 was 'embroidery.' In ancient times, cloth with embroidery was rare and hard to obtain. So 希 was extended to mean 'rare' and 'scarce.' In modern Chinese, 希 appears in a compound word with 望 ('to gaze into the distance') to mean 'hope; expectation; to hope; to expect.' Think of it this way: when you're hoping for something, it's like you're gazing into the future for something precious that is rare and scarce.

父母希望我以後能常常回去看望他們。	父母希望我以后能常常回去看望他们。
中國父母把孩子看作生活的希望。	中国父母把孩子看作生活的希望。
我希望我能上一所好大學。	我希望我能上一所好大学。
希望明天不會像今天這樣熱。	希望明天不会像今天这样热。

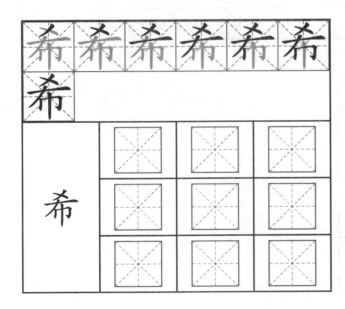

Unit 13 63

望 (*wàng*)

wàng	Ancient Form	Later Form	Modern Form
gaze into the distance; hope; expect	𦣞	望	望
xīwàng			希望

The original and still primary meaning of 望 is 'gaze into the distance.' The ancient form of 望 is a person with a big eye (目), in profile, standing on a mound. In the later form, the bottom mound became the character 土 (*tǔ*, 'earth, soil'), and a 月 (*yuè*, 'moon') was added, indicating 'looking from a long distance.' The modern form has 亡 (*wáng*) on the top left and 王 (*wáng*) at the bottom as two phonetic components. 月, on the top right, is the radical. When you are thinking or waiting or hoping, it's like you're 'gazing into the distance.' So 望 is extended to mean 'hope, expect.' 望 appears in compound words relating to 'gaze into the distance' or 'hope.' For example:

希望 rare + expect = 'hope'	望見/望见 to gaze into the distance + see = 'see from a distance'
期望 scheduled time + hope = 'expect; expectation'	看望 look + to gaze into the distance = 'pay a visit'

從山上望下去，看到的都是綠色。	从山上望下去，看到的都是绿色。
你父母希望你長大以後當什麼？	你父母希望你长大以后当什么？
中國父母對小孩的期望很高。	中国父母对小孩的期望很高。
我們應該常常找空去看望爺爺奶奶。	我们应该常常找空去看望爷爷奶奶。

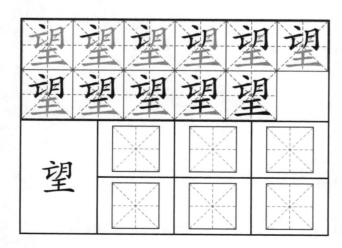

Copyright © 2012 by Yale University and China International Publishing Group

禮/礼 *(lǐ)*

lǐ	Ancient Form	Later Form	Modern Traditional Form	Modern Simplified Form
courtesy; ceremony; gift	豊	禮	禮	礼
lǐwù			禮物	礼物

The original form of this character is 豊 (*lǐ*). It is pretty much the same as the ancient form—a sketch of a tall container with something inside, representing the meaning 'vessel used in sacrificing.' Later, 示/礻 (*shì*, 'altar') was added to 豊 to form a new character 禮, meaning 'offering sacrifices to gods.' 示/礻 is the radical and 豊 (*lǐ*) is another signific component as well as the phonetic component. The modern simplified form replaces 豊 with a simple stroke, 乚.

示/礻 is a very important radical. It often appears in compound characters indicating 'religion,' 'ghosts and gods,' 'ancestry,' 'sacrificial rites,' or 'etiquette.' We have learned the following characters that use 示/礻 as a radical: 祝 (*zhù*, 'express good wishes'); 福 (*fú*, 'blessing; good fortune'); 神 (*shén*, 'god'). Can you list more?

禮/礼 appears in compound words relating to 'courtesy,' 'gift,' or 'ceremony.' For example:

婚禮/婚礼 marry + ceremony = 'wedding'	禮物/礼物 courtesy + thing = 'gift; present'
禮拜/礼拜 ceremony + do obeisance = 'religious service; week'	禮讓/礼让 courtesy + let; allow = 'give precedence to someone out of courtesy or thoughtfulness'

謝謝你送給我禮物。	谢谢你送给我礼物。
這個禮拜你忙不忙？一起喝咖啡怎麼樣？	这个礼拜你忙不忙？一起喝咖啡怎么样？
爸爸，你今年會給我買什麼生日禮物？	爸爸，你今年会给我买什么生日礼物？
有些人喜歡在夏天的時候辦婚禮。	有些人喜欢在夏天的时候办婚礼。

Modern Traditional Form	Modern Simplified Form

禮 禮 禮 禮 禮 禮
禮 禮 禮 禮 禮 禮
禮 禮 禮 禮 禮

礼 礼 礼 礼 礼

禮

礼

物 (wù)

wù	Ancient Form	Later Form	Modern Form
article; object; thing	牛	物	物
lǐwù			禮物/礼物

The original meaning of 物 was 'varicolored ox.' 牛 (*niú*, 'cow; ox') is the radical, indicating that the whole character is related to 'cow or ox.' 勿 (*wù*) is the phonetic component as well as another radical because it originally meant 'motley flag.' Since a 物 has various colors, it is extended to mean 'each and every thing in the world.' 物 appears in compound words relating to 'thing' or 'object.' For example:

物價/物价 thing + price = 'commodity price'	怪物 strange + thing = 'monster'
財物/财物 wealth + thing = 'property'	動物/动物 move + thing = 'animal'

我們應該帶甚麼禮物去看望爺爺奶奶？	我们应该带什么礼物去看望爷爷奶奶？
上海的物價比北京的物價高。	上海的物价比北京的物价高。
這山上有很多小動物。	这山上有很多小动物。
他來美國以前，把很多財物都送給了朋友。	他来美国以前，把很多财物都送给了朋友。

物 物 物 物 物 物
物 物

物

麻 (má)

má	Later Form	Modern Form
hemp (fiber); numbness; chaos	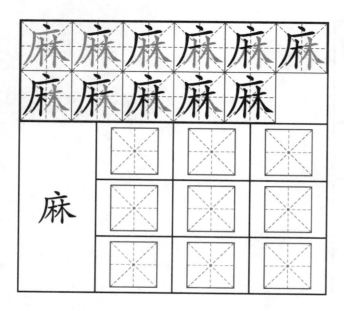	麻
máfan		麻煩/麻烦

麻 is formed with two signific components: 广 (*guǎng*, 'space') and double 木 (*mù*, 'tree'). The original meaning of 麻 was 'to make fiber out of hemp under a building.' In modern Chinese, 'hemp' is a still a primary meaning of 麻. Since making fiber, yarn, or rope out of hemp is very tedious and troublesome, 麻 is also used to mean 'troublesome,' 'chaos,' or 'pesky.' 麻 appears in compound words relating to 'hemp,' 'troublesome,' or 'numbness.' For example:

麻煩/麻烦 troublesome + annoy = 'bother; imposition'	麻油 hemp + oil = 'sesame oil'
麻木 tingle + wood = 'numb; numbness'	麻辣 tingle + hot; peppery = 'numbingly spicy'

麻煩你給我一杯水。	麻烦你给我一杯水。
四川菜是麻辣口味。	四川菜是麻辣口味。
太多太多的工作，我都麻木了。	太多太多的工作，我都麻木了。
中國人做菜喜歡用麻油。	中国人做菜喜欢用麻油。

Copyright © 2012 by Yale University and China International Publishing Group

fán	Later Form	Modern Traditional Form	Modern Simplified Form
be annoyed; be irritated	煩	煩	烦
máfan		麻煩	麻烦

煩/烦 is formed with two radicals, 火 (*huǒ*, 'fire') and 頁/页 (*yè*, 'head' when used as a radical). When you feel anxious or annoyed, don't you feel sweaty and hot? We learned that the 頁/页 radical means 'head' in Unit 11, when we learned the character 題/题. 煩/烦 appears in compound words relating to 'annoyance,' 'trouble,' or 'worry.' For example:

麻煩/麻烦 troublesome + annoy = 'troublesome; pesky'	心煩/心烦 heart + annoy = 'be vexed'
煩亂/烦乱 annoy + disorder = 'be upset'	煩人/烦人 annoy + person = 'irritating; annoying'

這件事很麻煩。	这件事很麻烦。
他找工作找了一年多，還沒找到，很心煩。	他找工作找了一年多，还没找到，很心烦。
這幾天工作很忙，家裡孩子又病了，我心裡很煩亂。	这几天工作很忙，家里孩子又病了，我心里很烦乱。
他說話總是很大聲，很煩人。	他说话总是很大声，很烦人。

Modern Traditional Form	Modern Simplified Form
煩 煩 煩 煩 煩 煩 煩 煩 煩 煩 煩 煩 煩	烦 烦 烦 烦 烦 烦 烦 烦 烦 烦
煩	烦

簡/简 (*jiǎn*)

jiǎn	Later Form	Modern Traditional Form	Modern Simplified Form
simple; brief	簡	簡	简
jiǎndān		簡單	简单

簡/简 is a picto-phonetic character. The original meaning of 簡/简 was 'bamboo slips.' The top part is 竹 (*zhú*, 'bamboo'), the radical. The bottom part is 間/间 (*jiān*), the phonetic component. (間/间 means 'gap.') In ancient times, people wrote on a lot of 簡/简 (bamboo slips) and then connected all the slips in order to make a book or letter. The book could be very heavy, and making a bamboo slip was cumbersome. So when one wrote, one tried to make a long story short to use fewer 簡/简. Therefore, 簡/简 gradually came to mean 'simple,' 'brief.' 簡/简 appears in compound words relating to 'simple,' 'brief.' For example:

簡單/简单 simple + single = 'simple; easy'	簡便/简便 simple + convenient = 'simple and convenient'
簡體字/简体字 simple + body + character = 'simplified Chinese characters'	簡要/简要 brief + important = 'concise'

你學的漢字是簡體字嗎?	你学的汉字是简体字吗?
這個問題很簡單。	这个问题很简单。
做飯看起來很簡單，做起來不簡單。	做饭看起来很简单，做起来不简单。
對學生的問題，他簡要地回答了一下。	对学生的问题，他简要地回答了一下。

Modern Traditional Form	Modern Simplified Form
簡 簡 簡 簡 簡 簡	简 简 简 简 简 简
簡 簡 簡 簡 簡 簡	简 简 简 简 简 简
簡 簡 簡 簡 簡 簡	简

簡					简			

單/单 (*dān*)

dān	Ancient Form	Later Form	Modern Traditional Form	Modern Simplified Form
single; alone; simple	単	單	單	单
jiǎndān			簡單	简单

單/单 originally was a simple hunting tool or weapon made with a tree branch and two stones bound on the two ends of the fork. Later it was extended to mean 'single,' 'simple,' 'alone.' 單/单 appears in compound words relating to 'single,' 'simple,' or 'alone.' For example:

單調/单调 single + tone = 'monotonous; dull'	單一/单一 single + one = 'monotonous'
單衣/单衣 simple + clothes = 'unlined garment'	單車/单车 simple + vehicle = 'bicycle'

每天都做同樣的事，生活真單調。	每天都做同样的事，生活真单调。
他說簡單的生活就是讓人高興的生活。	他说简单的生活就是让人高兴的生活。
有些地方把自行車叫單車。	有些地方把自行车叫单车。
媽媽說我吃的東西太單一，應該吃很多不同的蔬菜、肉和水果。	妈妈说我吃的东西太单一，应该吃很多不同的蔬菜、肉和水果。

Modern Traditional Form	Modern Simplified Form
單 單 單 單 單 單 單 單 單 單 單 單 單	单 单 单 单 单 单 单 单 单

帶 / 带 (dài)

dài	Ancient Form	Later Form	Modern Traditional Form	Modern Simplified Form
belt; bring along	帶	帶	帶	带
dài lǐwù gěi péngyou			帶禮物給朋友	带礼物给朋友

The original meaning of 帶/带 was 'belt.' The top part is a sketch of a belt wrapped around a waist. The two endings with knots are hanging for decoration. The bottom part, 巾 (*jīn*, 'a piece of cloth'), indicates that the whole character is related to cloth. Since a belt is used to attach something to the body, 帶/带 was extended to mean 'to bring along.' 帶/带 appears in compound words relating to 'belt' or 'bring.' For example:

帶好/带好 bring + good = 'say hello to'	帶路/带路 bring + road = 'lead the way'
地帶/地带 earth + belt = 'zone; area'	帶頭/带头 bring + head = 'pioneer; be the first'

他很喜歡我帶給他的禮物。	他很喜欢我带给他的礼物。
請為我給你的父母帶好。	请为我给你的父母带好。
他聰明又能幹，總是第一個帶頭做事。	他聪明又能干，总是第一个带头做事。
你去過那個公園，你在前面帶路吧。	你去过那个公园，你在前面带路吧。

Modern Traditional Form	Modern Simplified Form
帶 帶 帶 帶 帶 帶 帶 帶 帶 帶 帶 帶	带 带 带 带 带 带 带 带 带
帶	带

送 *(sòng)*

sòng	Later Form	Modern Form
see someone off; give as a gift	𧗲	送
sòng lǐwù		送禮物／送礼物

The original meaning of 送 was to 'accompany the bride to the groom's family on the wedding day.' The left part of the later form is 辵 ('foot on road'), indicating that the whole character is related to walking. It has 火 ('fire') at the top right and 'hands' at the bottom right, because, in ancient times, the bride was sent to the groom's family in the evening when it was dark. Gradually the semantic compass of 送 was extended to people and objects other than brides. The modern form uses 辶 (the simplified form of 辵) to indicate 'distance.' 关 here is just a symbol, not a signific or phonetic component. Incidentally, 关 (*guān*) is the modern simplified form of 關, meaning 'shut; close.' To help you remember, you can associate 送 with 'closing your door after you see your guests off.' 送 appears in compound words relating to 'send,' 'see someone off,' or 'deliver.' For example:

歡送／欢送 joyous + see someone off = 'bid farewell to someone'	送客 see someone off + guest = 'see a visitor out'
送禮／送礼 deliver + gift = 'present a gift to someone'	送走 send + go = 'send someone or something away'

你送給你爸爸媽媽新年禮物嗎？	你送给你爸爸妈妈新年礼物吗？
我們晚上十點多把客人都送走了。	我们晚上十点多把客人都送走了。
中國人送客的時候要和客人一起走到門外。	中国人送客的时候要和客人一起走到门外。

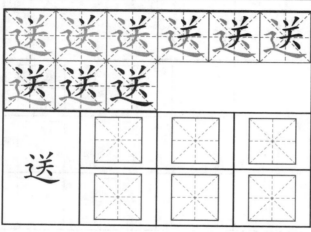

然 (*rán*)

rán	Later Form	Modern Form
right; so; like that; however	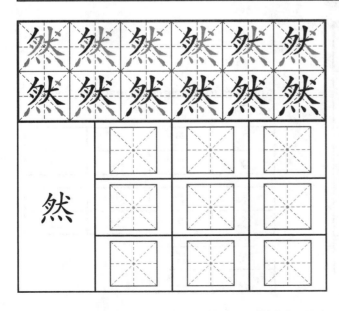	然
ránhòu		然後/然后

然 originally meant 'to burn.' 火/灬 (*huǒ*, 'fire') at the bottom is the radical, indicating that the whole character is related to 'fire.' The top left is a symbol of a piece of meat. The top right is 犬 (*quǎn*, 'dog'). Why is there a 犬 here? Maybe it indicates the meat is dog meat, or maybe it indicates that the meat is from a dog's hunting. 然 meaning 'right; correct; however' is a phonetic loan. The original meaning of 'to burn' is now represented by a new character, 燃, which was created by adding 火 to 然. 然 appears in compound words, especially in pronouns or conjunction words relating to 'right,' 'but,' 'so,' or 'still.' For example:

當然/当然 equal + right = 'of course'	然後/然后 right + after = 'then; afterwards'
果然 fruit + so = 'as expected; really'	自然 self + so = 'nature; natural'

我現在要去上課，然後回家。	我现在要去上课，然后回家。
他果然是我們老師的男朋友。	他果然是我们老师的男朋友。
要是你去看電影，你的孩子當然也想去。	要是你去看电影，你的孩子当然也想去。
這個外國學生說中文說得很自然。	这个外国学生说中文说得很自然。

真 (*zhēn*)

zhēn	Later Form	Modern Form
real; true; genuine	眞	真
Zhè ge zhēn hǎochī!		這個真好吃！/ 这个真好吃！

真 was a Taoist term, referring to the Immortals who grasp the truth. They are called 真人 (*zhēnrén*). In the later form, 匕 means 'change,' indicating those 真人 change their forms and go to heaven. 目 means 'eye,' and 乚 means 'hide,' indicating that common people can't see 真人 unless they want you to. 八 at the bottom represents a tool to carry 真人. Usually the tool is a cloud. From 真人, 真 has been extended to mean 'true,' 'real,' and 'genuine.' 真 appears in compound words relating to 'true,' 'real,' and 'genuine.' For example:

真心 true + heart = 'sincere'	真心真意 true + heart + true + meaning = 'sincere; honest'
真正 true + central; just = 'true'	真知 true + know = 'genuine knowledge'

他真心真意請你去他家做客。	他真心真意请你去他家做客。
你真的要去中國嗎？	你真的要去中国吗？
你的中文學得真好！說得真自然！	你的中文学得真好！说得真自然！
美國的中國菜都是酸甜口味，不是真正的中國菜。	美国的中国菜都是酸甜口味，不是真正的中国菜。

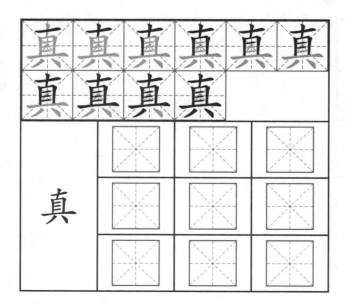

Answers to the Seven Questions exercise (p. 57):

浪	葡	梨	一
氵	艹	木	一

衣	音	基	因
衣	音	土	口

劫	匹
力	匚

Unit 14

The sentences below are inspired by the contents of Unit 14 and contain all the new characters required for writing as well as others. Read and reread until fluent, covering the English as you read. Then cover the English and try to reproduce the Chinese equivalents orally. Do this exercise before beginning to practice writing.

這家廣東餐館的菜味道真好。 这家广东餐馆的菜味道真好。	The food in this Cantonese restaurant is very tasty.
麻婆豆腐是一道很有名的川菜。	Mapo tofu is a very famous Sichuan dish.
天氣太熱了，來杯冰奶茶或是冰可樂吧。 天气太热了，来杯冰奶茶或是冰可乐吧。	It's too hot; how about a glass of ice milk tea or soda with some ice?
蛋炒飯是我最喜歡的家常菜。 蛋炒饭是我最喜欢的家常菜。	Fried rice with scrambled eggs is my favorite home-style food.
中國南方人常吃米飯，北方人常吃麵。 中国南方人常吃米饭，北方人常吃面。	Southerners in China eat steamed rice regularly, whereas northerners eat noodles regularly.
你需要甚麼就跟我说，別太客氣。 你需要什么就跟我说，别太客气。	If you need something, let me know; don't be too polite.
橘子汁酸酸甜甜的，很好喝。	Orange juice is sour and sweet; it's delicious.
明天我們一同去天安門廣場看看。 明天我们一同去天安门广场看看。	Tomorrow, let's go together to visit Tiananmen Square.
主人對客人说：請上桌，隨便坐。 主人对客人说：请上桌，随便坐。	The host said to the guests, 'Please come to the table; sit wherever you like.'

Practice with Radicals and Phonetics

Here's a bunch of characters drawn from lessons you've already covered. Try your hand at identifying the radical and the phonetic of each. Recall the 'Seven Questions,' your key to locating the radical? For review, here they are again, put a bit differently.

> The 'Seven Questions': Is the radical on the *top, bottom, left, right*? Does the radical *enclose* the character? Is the radical a character in itself (*all*)? Does the character have one *lone* radical?

If you recognize the radical, do your best to recall its meaning. And recall that the simplification process has altered the shape and location of radicals. Some characters have even lost their original radical, whereas others have 'switched' radicals. I know, a real pain. You will find examples of all these below.

And the phonetic? Well, it's usually on the right side of the character. That 'rule' should suffice for now. But also keep in mind that although most characters have a phonetic component, not all do.

Have fun. Work with a partner if possible. Identify as many radicals and phonetics as you can. Good luck!

	radical	phonetic		radical	phonetic
紅/红			週/周		
姐			字		
口			遠/远		
餓/饿			銀/银		
吧			早		
個/个			這/这		
到			請/请		
裡/里			了		
忙			一		
們/们			時/时		
念			影		

餐 (cān)

cān	Later Form	Modern Form
meal; food	𣊟	餐
chī Zhōngcān		吃中餐

The bottom part of 餐 is 食 (*shí*). It looks like a food container with a person at the top. 食, the radical, means 'food; eat.' The top part of 餐 used to be the phonetic component, but it no longer is. 歺 on the top left looks like a bone. We already learned that 又 (on the top right) represents 'hand' in compound characters. When you have a meal, you need to use a food container and hands, and you love ribs, right? 餐 appears in compound words relating to 'food,' 'meal.' For example:

快餐 quick + meal = 'fast food'	餐巾 meal + cloth = 'cloth napkin'
西餐 west + meal = 'Western-style food'	餐桌 meal + table = 'dining table'

餐桌上有餐巾、杯子，還有水果。	餐桌上有餐巾、杯子，还有水果。
你喜歡吃中餐還是西餐？	你喜欢吃中餐还是西餐？
美國的中餐館很多。	美国的中餐馆很多。
你常常吃西方的快餐嗎？	你常常吃西方的快餐吗？

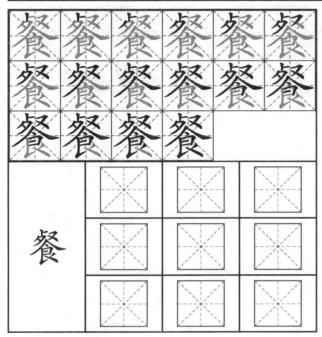

館/馆 (guǎn)

guǎn	Later Form	Modern Traditional Form	Modern Simplified Form
(guesthouse)	舘	館	馆
cānguǎn		餐館	餐馆

館/馆 originally meant 'accommodation for guests.' 食/饣 (*shí*, 'to eat; food') on the left and 宀 (roof of a house) on the top right are both radicals. Understandably, a guesthouse must provide meals. 官 (*guān*, 'official') is the phonetic component. In modern Chinese, 館/馆 was expanded to mean 'a public space for food, lodging, cultural activities, etc.' For example:

飯館/饭馆 food + guesthouse = 'restaurant'	咖啡館/咖啡馆 coffee + guesthouse = 'café'
茶館/茶馆 tea + guesthouse= 'teahouse'	圖書館/图书馆 chart; picture + book + guesthouse = 'library'

我不在家裡請客，總是在飯館請客。	我不在家里请客，总是在饭馆请客。
以前這裡沒有咖啡館，只有茶館。	以前这里没有咖啡馆，只有茶馆。
你喜歡什麼樣的餐館？	你喜欢什么样的餐馆？

Modern Traditional Form	Modern Simplified Form
館 館 館 館 館 館 館 館 館 館 館 館 館 館 館 館	馆 馆 馆 馆 馆 馆 馆 馆 馆 馆 馆

安 (ān)

ān	Ancient Form	Later Form	Modern Form
safe; peaceful			安
Xī'ān			西安

安 is formed with a 女 (*nǚ*, 'woman') under 宀 ('roof of a house'), representing 'safe, peaceful.' A woman feels safe and peaceful inside a building (home). 安 appears in compound words relating to 'safe,' 'peaceful,' or 'stable.' For example:

安心 peaceful + heart = 'reassuring; reassured'	晚安 night + safe = 'good night'
安定 safe + still = 'stable'	公安 public + safe = 'public safety'

聽到孩子回來了，媽媽才安心去睡覺。	听到孩子回来了，妈妈才安心去睡觉。
每天睡覺前，我都對父母說'晚安'。	每天睡觉前，我都对父母说'晚安'。
我希望過一個簡單、安定的生活。	我希望过一个简单、安定的生活。
西安是一個很有意思的城市。	西安是一个很有意思的城市。

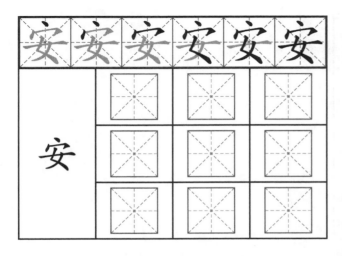

同 (*tóng*)

tóng	Ancient Form	Later Form	Modern Form
same; common	𐂇	同	同
bùtóng			不同

The ancient form of 同 was formed with a 凡 (*fán*, 'every; all') covering a 口 (*kǒu*, 'mouth'), signifying that all the people have the same voice. So the original meaning of 同 was 'common' or 'resemblance.' Here's a memory aid for you: within the boundary (冂 means 'boundary'), there is just one (一) voice (口), indicating that everyone is in common agreement with one another. 同 was later extended to mean 'equal,' 'identical,' 'agree,' and 'together.' See the following compound words:

不同 not + same = 'different'	同學/同学 together + study = 'classmate'
同事 together + thing = 'colleague'	同時/同时 same + time = 'at the same time'

中國不同地方的菜的做法和口味也不同。	中国不同地方的菜的做法和口味也不同。
他以前是我的同學，現在是我的同事。	他以前是我的同学，现在是我的同事。
我和哥哥同時開始學習中文。	我和哥哥同时开始学习中文。
不同的學生有不同的學習方法。	不同的学生有不同的学习方法。

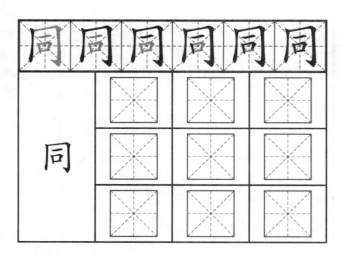

chuān	Ancient Form	Later Form	Modern Form
river	〰〰〰	川	川
Zhōngguó Sìchuān			中國四川/中国四川

川 is a pictographic character. Can you see the wave-shaped river water? 川 means 'river' and is also extended to mean 'valley.' Can you guess how 四川 ('Sichuan Province') got its name? 川 appears in a few compound words in idioms relating to 'river' or 'Sichuan Province.' For example:

名山大川 name + mountain + big + river = 'famous mountains and great rivers'	川菜 Sichuan + dishes = 'Sichuan cuisine'
一马平川 one + horse + flat + river = 'a wide expanse of flat land'	川劇/川剧 Sichuan + drama = 'Sichuan opera'

川菜很辣，你喜歡吃川菜嗎？	川菜很辣，你喜欢吃川菜吗？
我喜歡去看名山大川，我哥哥喜歡去看不同的城市。	我喜欢去看名山大川，我哥哥喜欢去看不同的城市。
這家川菜館的菜味道很好。	这家川菜馆的菜味道很好。
美國的名山大川你都看過嗎？	美国的名山大川你都看过吗？

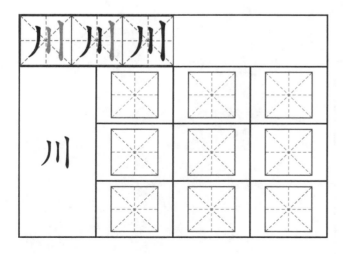

汁 (*zhī*)

zhī	Later Form	Modern Form
juice	〴十	汁
guǒzhī		果汁

You might not need help remembering this character. 汁 is a very straightforward picto-phonetic character meaning 'the liquid contained in something that is solid.' 水/氵, on the left, is the radical, indicating that the whole character is related to 'water' or 'liquid.' 十 (*shí*, 'ten'), on the right, is the phonetic component.

你喜歡喝哪種果汁?	你喜欢喝哪种果汁?
我覺得蘋果汁最好喝。	我觉得苹果汁最好喝。
新鮮的果菜汁又營養又好喝。	新鲜的果菜汁又营养又好喝。
上海口味的包子裡有很多肉汁。	上海口味的包子里有很多肉汁。

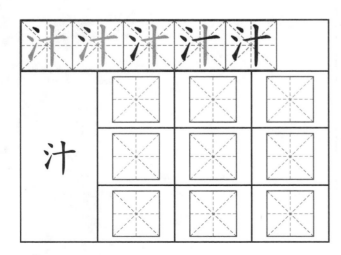

kě	Ancient Form	Later Form	Modern Form
may; can; but; be worthy of	丂	可	可
kěyǐ			可以

The original meaning of 可 was 'to allow, to approve.' 口 (*kǒu*, 'mouth') is the radical, indicating that the whole character is related to speech (and by extension, oral permission). 可 is also used to mean 'be worthy of,' 'may,' 'can,' or 'but.' Note that 可樂/可乐 is a transliteration of 'cola.' 可 here is just a phonetic symbol. 可 is a very useful character to learn. It appears in many compound words. For example:

可愛/可爱 be worthy of + love = 'adorable'	可見/可见 may + see = 'it is obvious that'
可貴/可贵 be worthy of + expensive; costly = 'admirable'	可以 may + use = 'may; can'
可笑 be worthy of + laugh = 'ridiculous; funny'	可能 may + ability = 'possible; possibility'
可喜 be worthy of + happy = 'gratifying'	可是 but + be = 'but; however'

這個小孩子真可愛。	这个小孩子真可爱。
他喜歡吃川菜，可是這裡沒有川菜館。	他喜欢吃川菜，可是这里没有川菜馆。
我可以用一下你的書嗎？	我可以用一下你的书吗？
他可能是中國人，也可能是日本人。	他可能是中国人，也可能是日本人。

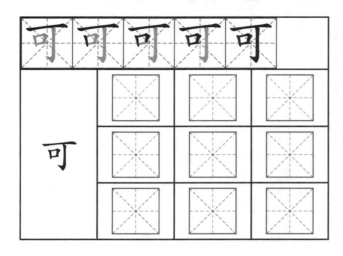

lè	Ancient Form	Later Form	Modern Traditional Form	Modern Simplified Form
music; happy; joy			樂	乐
kělè			可樂	可乐

樂/乐 originally meant 'musical instrument' and 'music.' The ancient form is 木 (*mù*, 'tree, wood'), with 幺 (*sī*, 'silk') at the top to indicate musical instruments, such as a seven-stringed zither. The strings of these instruments are made of silk. Since music can bring one happiness and joy, 樂/乐 is extended to mean 'happy,' 'glad,' or 'joy.' Note that 樂/乐 is pronounced *yuè* when it means 'music' and *lè* when it means 'happy,' 'glad,' or 'joy.' For example:

音樂/音乐 (*yuè*) sound + music = 'music'	樂感/乐感 (*yuè*) music + sense; feel = 'one's musical sense'
快樂/快乐 (*lè*) quick + happy = 'happy; joyful'	樂器/乐器 (*yuè*) music + gadget = 'musical instrument'

你玩什麼樂器？你的樂感那麼好。	你玩什么乐器？你的乐感那么好。
他每天看起來都很快樂。	他每天看起来都很快乐。
你喜歡聽什麼樣的音樂？	你喜欢听什么样的音乐？

Modern Traditional Form	Modern Simplified Form

Copyright © 2012 by Yale University and China International Publishing Group

奶 (nǎi)

nǎi	Later Form	Modern Form
milk	奶	奶
hē niúnǎi		喝牛奶

奶 is a picto-phonetic character. 女 (nǔ, 'woman'), on the left, is the radical, indicating that the whole character is related to 'woman' or 'female.' 乃 (nǎi), on the right, is the phonetic component, representing the pronunciation of the whole character accurately. The original meaning of 奶 was 'breast.' In modern Chinese, 奶 is often used to mean 'milk,' 'to milk.' Note that 奶奶 (pronounced nǎinai) means 'paternal grandmother.' 奶 appears in compound words relating to 'milk.' For example:

奶茶 milk + tea = 'tea with milk'	奶牛 milk + cow = 'milk cow'
豆奶 bean + milk = 'soy milk'	酸奶 sour + milk = 'yogurt'

你喝咖啡的時候加牛奶嗎？	你喝咖啡的时候加牛奶吗？
如果奶牛每天聽音樂，牛奶會更好喝。	如果奶牛每天听音乐，牛奶会更好喝。
我不喜歡喝牛奶，我吃酸奶。	我不喜欢喝牛奶，我吃酸奶。
在中國，每天喝豆奶的人很多。	在中国，每天喝豆奶的人很多。

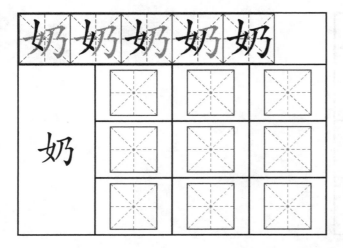

冰 (*bīng*)

bīng	Later Form	Modern Form
ice	仌巛	冰
bīngshuǐ		冰水

冰 associates water and ice. 仌, on the left in the later form, is a sketch of ice piles. In the modern form, 仌 is written as 冫, which is a very important radical meaning 'ice.' 水 (*shuǐ*, 'water'), on the right, is another radical indicating that the whole character is related to 'water.' It's important to differentiate 氵 ('water') from 冫 ('ice'). 冰 appears in compound words relating to 'ice,' 'cold,' or 'frost.' For example:

冰山 ice + mountain = 'iceberg'	冰川 ice + river = 'glacier'
冰球 ice + ball = 'ice hockey'	結冰/结冰 form + ice = 'freeze'

我喜歡喝冰水、冰茶或者冰牛奶。	我喜欢喝冰水、冰茶或者冰牛奶。
現在冰山變得越來越小，越來越少了。	现在冰山变得越来越小，越来越少了。
你喜歡玩冰球嗎？	你喜欢玩冰球吗？
今天真冷，已經結冰了，冬天來了。	今天真冷，已经结冰了，冬天来了。

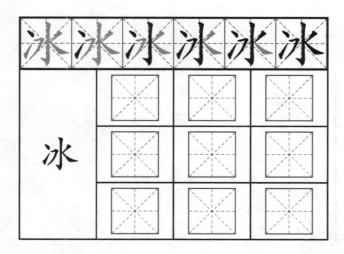

Copyright © 2012 by Yale University and China International Publishing Group

豆 (dòu)

dòu	Ancient Form	Later Form	Modern Form
bean	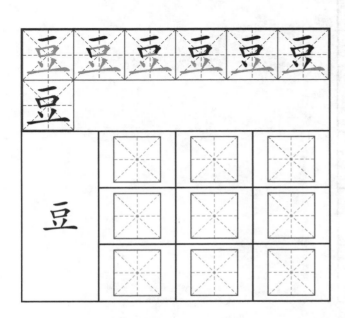		豆
dòunǎi			豆奶

豆 originally meant 'a container of food used in sacrificial ceremonies.' The ancient form was a sketch of a container with a tall stand. 豆 was used as a phonetic loan for 'bean' after the Han Dynasty. Gradually the original meaning was dropped. 豆 appears in compound words relating to 'bean' or 'bean shaped.' For example:

咖啡豆 coffee + bean = 'coffee bean'	豆奶 bean + milk = 'soy milk'
土豆 soil + bean = 'potato'	黄豆 yellow + bean = 'soybean'

美國人很喜歡吃炸土豆條。	美国人很喜欢吃炸土豆条。
我今天買了黃豆、紅豆、綠豆、黑豆。	我今天买了黄豆、红豆、绿豆、黑豆。
我最喜歡的家常菜是麻婆豆腐。	我最喜欢的家常菜是麻婆豆腐。
你喝冰豆奶還是熱豆奶？	你喝冰豆奶还是热豆奶？

豆 豆 豆 豆 豆 豆
豆

豆

腐 (fǔ)

fǔ	Later Form	Modern Form
rotten; corrupted	腐	腐
dòufu		豆腐

腐 is a picto-phonetic character. 府 (*fǔ*), at the top, is the phonetic component. 肉 (*ròu*, 'meat') is the radical, indicating that the whole character is related to 'meat.' The original meaning was 'rotten meat.' Gradually 腐 became used to mean 'anything that becomes rotten.' The reason why 腐 is used in the word 豆腐 ('bean curd') is because during the production process of bean curd, the beans look like they're rotten. Note that 腐 in 豆腐 is neutral tone.

我喜歡吃麻婆豆腐，我想學會怎麼做。	我喜欢吃麻婆豆腐，我想学会怎么做。
這個菜叫什錦豆腐，又好看又好吃。	这个菜叫什锦豆腐，又好看又好吃。
中國人都覺得多吃豆腐對身體好。	中国人都觉得多吃豆腐对身体好。
杏仁豆腐看起來像豆腐，但不是用豆腐做的。	杏仁豆腐看起来像豆腐，但不是用豆腐做的。

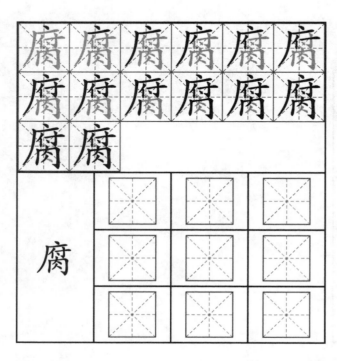

米 (mǐ)

mǐ	Ancient Form	Later Form	Modern Form
uncooked rice; a shelled or husked seed	⫲⫲	米	米
mǐfàn			米飯／米饭

米 is a pictographic character. The ancient form had scattered dots indicating grains of rice and a horizontal stroke indicating a sieve. In the later and modern forms this horizontal stroke became 十. 米 is a very important radical used as a component in many characters related to 'rice' or 'rice shaped.' 米 appears in a few compound words relating to 'rice.' For example:

米湯／米汤 rice + soup = 'thin rice or millet gruel'	米飯／米饭 rice + meal = 'cooked rice'
米色 rice + color = 'cream colored'	米酒 rice + wine = 'rice wine'

你要炒米飯還是白米飯？	你要炒米饭还是白米饭？
中國南方人吃很多米飯。	中国南方人吃很多米饭。
我喜歡這件米色的衣服。	我喜欢这件米色的衣服。
炒菜的時候放一點兒米酒，味道會更香。	炒菜的时候放一点儿米酒，味道会更香。

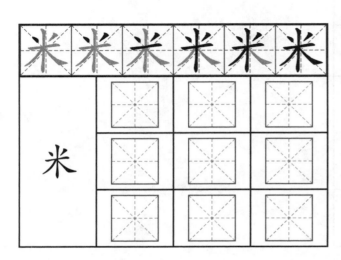

炒 (*chǎo*)

chǎo	Later Form	Modern Form
stir-fry	火少	炒
chǎo mǐfàn		炒米飯/炒米饭

You can tell that 炒 is a picto-phonetic character, right? 火 (*huǒ*, 'fire'), on the left, is the radical. 少 (*shǎo*), on the right, is the phonetic component. *Shǎo* and *chǎo* share the same tone and the same final *ao*. Here is a bonus for you: 吵 (*chǎo*), with a 口 ('mouth') along with 少, means 'noisy' or 'making noise.'

晚飯有炒米飯、炒菠菜，還有麻婆豆腐。	晚饭有炒米饭、炒菠菜，还有麻婆豆腐。
美國人常常烤東西吃，中國人喜歡炒菜吃。	美国人常常烤东西吃，中国人喜欢炒菜吃。
請給我來一盤蛋炒飯。	请给我来一盘蛋炒饭。
我不喜歡吃湯麵，我喜歡吃炒麵。	我不喜欢吃汤面，我喜欢吃炒面。

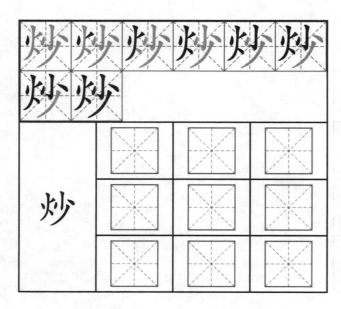

miàn	Later Form	Modern Traditional Form	Modern Simplified Form
flour; dough	麵	麵	面
chǎomiàn		炒麵	炒面

The character 面 ('face') is not new to you. We learned 面 in Unit 10. You can see 目 ('eye') inside the outline of a face. Later 面 was extended to mean 'surface,' 'side,' or 'aspect,' as in words such as 外面, 上面, 下面. 麵／面 meaning 'flour' is a phonetic loan. The traditional form 麵 is a picto-phonetic character. 麥 (*mài*, 'wheat'), on the left, is the radical, and 面, on the right, is the phonetic component. The simplified form retains the phonetic component but deletes the radical. 麵／面 meaning 'flour' or 'dough' doesn't appear in many compound words. Here are a few:

炒麵／炒面 stir-fry + noodle = 'fried noodles'	麵條／面条 flour + strip = 'noodles'
湯麵／汤面 soup + noodle = 'noodles in soup'	麵食／面食 flour + food = 'staple foods made from flour'

中國北方人吃很多麵食，南方人吃很多米飯。	中国北方人吃很多面食，南方人吃很多米饭。
明天我要在家裡請客，今天我買了很多麵條、蔬菜和肉。	明天我要在家里请客，今天我买了很多面条、蔬菜和肉。
你喜歡吃湯面還是炒麵？	你喜欢吃汤面还是炒面？
這家餐館的麵條做得很好吃。	这家餐馆的面条做得很好吃。

Modern Traditional Form	Modern Simplified Form

麵 麵 麵 麵 麵 麵
麵 麵 麵 麵 麵 麵
麵 麵 麵 麵 麵 麵
麵 麵

面 面 面 面 面 面
面 面 面

麵

面

蛋 (dàn)

dàn	Later Form	Modern Form
egg	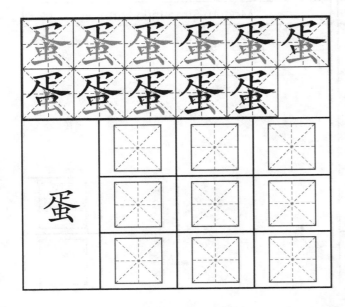 蛋	蛋
jīdàn		鸡蛋/雞蛋

蛋 means 'an egg of insects, snakes, or small animals.' 虫 (chóng, 'insects, snakes, or small animals'), at the bottom, is the radical. The top part is 疋, meaning 'foot.' Why is there a foot in the character 蛋? We don't know. Use your imagination to guess. In modern Chinese, 蛋 by itself usually means 'chicken egg,' unless modified by other characters. 蛋 appears in a few compound words relating to 'egg' or 'egg-shaped thing.' For example:

蛋白 egg + white = 'egg white'	蛋黄 egg + yellow = 'egg yolk'
鴨蛋/鸭蛋 duck + egg = 'duck egg'	臉蛋/脸蛋 face + egg-shaped thing = 'cheek'

鹹雞蛋的蛋黃很好吃。	咸鸡蛋的蛋黄很好吃。
我喜歡喝咖啡，吃蛋塔。	我喜欢喝咖啡，吃蛋塔。
這個小孩子的臉蛋紅紅的，很可愛。	这个小孩子的脸蛋红红的，很可爱。
每年生日的時候，我媽媽都給我做一個生日蛋糕。	每年生日的时候，我妈妈都给我做一个生日蛋糕。

廣/广 (*guǎng*)

guǎng	Ancient Form	Later Form	Modern Traditional Form	Modern Simplified Form
broad; vast; spacious	介	廣	廣	广
Guǎngdōng			廣東	广东

The ancient form of this character is a sketch of a simple building. The original meaning of 广 was 'a wall-less hall,' 'a shelter.' A wall-less hall usually feels 'spacious,' therefore, this character was extended to mean 'vast,' 'broad,' or 'spacious.' The original meaning was later dropped. The phonetic component 黃 (*huáng*) was added in the later form and kept in the modern traditional form. The modern simplified form dropped 黃. 廣/广 is often used in place names indicating 'broad.' It also appears in a few compound words. For example:

廣東/广东 broad + east = 'Guangdong Province'	廣大/广大 broad + big = 'vast'
廣告/广告 broad + to tell = 'advertisement'	廣場/广场 broad + field = 'square; plaza'

廣東、廣西在中國的南部。	广东、广西在中国的南部。
我覺得看電視廣告也很有意思。	我觉得看电视广告也很有意思。
你去過天安門廣場嗎？	你去过天安门广场吗？

Modern Traditional Form	Modern Simplified Form
廣 廣 廣 廣 廣 廣 廣 廣 廣 廣 廣 廣 廣 廣 廣	广 广 广
廣	广

96   *Unit 14*

Copyright © 2012 by Yale University and China International Publishing Group

就 (jiù)

jiù	Later Form	Modern Form
as soon as; as early as; right away; only	隷	就
Tā jiù hē le yì bēi chá.		他就喝了一杯茶。

With 就 (jiù), we encounter a character very important in understanding grammatical relationships within a sentence. 就 has many flavors—more than we can cover here. Most important, it serves as an adverb, as the examples below illustrate. Regarding the structure of the character, you might recall the left half as 京 (jīng), meaning 'capital.' Do you recognize these famous capitals: 北京, 南京, 東京/东京? By the way, the right half of 就 is 尤 (yóu), and together with the character 其 (qí), we have a very handy compound word 尤其, meaning 'especially.' Can you guess the meaning of this sentence? 這個地方天氣常常不好, 尤其是冬天的時候。/ 这个地方天气常常不好, 尤其是冬天的时候。

他吃完飯就走了。	他吃完饭就走了。	'as soon as'
我八點就來了。	我八点就来了。	'as early as'
你再等幾分鐘, 晚飯很快就做好了。	你再等几分钟, 晚饭很快就做好了。	'right away'
我們就要兩杯咖啡。	我们就要两杯咖啡。	'only'

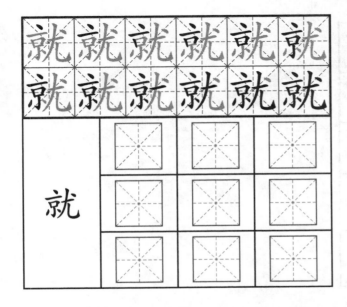

需 (xū)

xū	Ancient Form	Later Form	Modern Form
need; needs	术	需	需
xūyào			需要

The ancient form of 需 looks like a person in rain, representing the idea of 'delay and awaiting because of rain.' Therefore, the original meaning of 需 was 'awaiting.' The image in the ancient form became 而 in the later form, and 雨 (yǔ, 'rain') was added as another radical and phonetic component. If one is 'awaiting,' it means one wants or needs something. Therefore, 需 was extended to mean 'need(s),' 'necessities.' The original meaning of 'awaiting' was dropped. 需 appears in a few compound words relating to 'need.' For example:

需求 need + demand = 'requirement; demand'	必需 must + need = 'necessary'
需要 need + want = 'need; needs'	急需 urgent + need = 'be badly in need of'

你需要我什麼時候做好晚飯?	你需要我什么时候做好晚饭?
要是你有什麼需要，請告訴我。	要是你有什么需要，请告诉我。
要學好中文，每天練習是必需的。	要学好中文，每天练习是必需的。
我現在急需錢，你能幫我嗎?	我现在急需钱，你能帮我吗?

Copyright © 2012 by Yale University and China International Publishing Group

隨/随 (suí)

suí	Later Form	Modern Traditional Form	Modern Simplified Form
follow; comply with; adapt to	隨	隨	随
suíbiàn		隨便	随便

The original meaning of 隨/随 was 'to follow.' The left part, 阝, means 'wall,' 'town.' The middle part, 辵/辶, is a familiar radical you have learned before. It represents 'foot on road,' meaning 'walk,' 'travel.' Can you tell that the right part of this character includes 月 (*yuè*, meaning 'meat' here), 工 (*gōng*, 'work; worker'), and a left hand? So maybe the idea of this character was 'a worker (a butcher maybe?) with meat in his hand following someone on foot to town (for a delivery)'? From the meaning 'to follow,' 隨/随 was extended to mean 'follow one's will,' 'comply with,' 'adapt to.' 隨/随 appears in compound words relating to 'follow,' 'adapt to.' For example:

聽隨/听随 listen + follow = 'obey'	隨同/随同 follow + same = 'accompany'
隨時/随时 adapt to + time = 'at any time'	隨便/随便 adapt to + convenience = 'as one pleases'

我明天在家，你隨時都可以來看我。	我明天在家，你随时都可以来看我。
中國父母常對小孩兒説，到別人家裡做客，不可以太隨便。	中国父母常对小孩儿说，到别人家里做客，不可以太随便。
我隨同父母去看望他們的老朋友。	我随同父母去看望他们的老朋友。
別客氣，隨便坐。	别客气，随便坐。

Modern Traditional Form	Modern Simplified Form

隨 隨 隨 隨 隨 隨
隨 隨 隨 隨 隨 隨
隨 隨 隨 隨

随 随 随 随 随 随
随 随 随 随 随

隨

随

cháng	Later Form	Modern Form
frequently; constant; ordinary	常	常
jiāchángcài		家常菜

The original meaning of 常 was 'a skirt that one wears or sees frequently because it is popular.' The top part 尚 (*shàng*) is the phonetic component. 巾 (*jīn*, 'cloth') at the bottom is the radical, indicating that the whole character is related to 'cloth.' From the meaning of 'clothing you see or wear frequently,' 常 was extended to mean 'constant,' 'frequently,' and 'ordinary.' The original meaning of clothing has been dropped and is now represented by a new character, 裳 (*cháng*; *shang*). Note that the bottom part of 裳 is 衣 (*yī*, 'clothing'). Differentiate: 帶/带 (Unit 13), 常, 裳. 常 often appears in compound words relating to 'constant,' 'often,' or 'ordinary.' For example:

家常 home + constant = 'domestic; the daily life of a family'	日常 day + constant = 'daily'
常識/常识 ordinary + knowledge = 'common sense'	常見/常见 often + see = 'usual; common'

水冷了，就會變成冰，這是每個人都知道的常識。	水冷了，就会变成冰，这是每个人都知道的常识。
爸爸想聽你説説你在學校的日常生活。	爸爸想听你说说你在学校的日常生活。
現在中國餐館在美國很常見。	现在中国餐馆在美国很常见。
我們就點幾個家常菜吧。	我们就点几个家常菜吧。

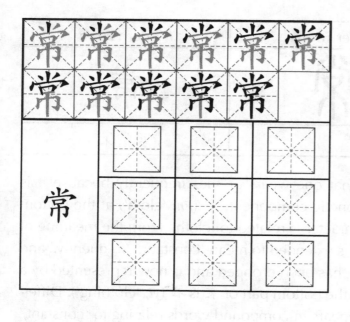

Unit 15

The sentences below are inspired by the contents of Unit 15 and contain all the new characters required for writing as well as others. Read and reread until fluent, covering the English as you read. Then cover the English and try to reproduce the Chinese equivalents orally. Do this exercise before beginning to practice writing.

我和同事約好下班以後去打球。 我和同事约好下班以后去打球。	I made an appointment with my colleague to play a ball game after work.
她没有工作，她還在讀書。 她没有工作，她还在读书。	She doesn't have a job; she's still attending school.
放學以後，我喜歡去外面跑步。 放学以后，我喜欢去外面跑步。	After school, I like to go running outside.
他很會唱歌，希望將來做個歌星。 他很会唱歌，希望将来做个歌星。	He sings very well; he hopes to become a singing star in the future.
閒下來的時間，我喜歡在家裡聽音樂。 闲下来的时间，我喜欢在家里听音乐。	In my free time, I like to listen to music at home.
越來越多人喜歡放假的時候到國外旅遊。 越来越多人喜欢放假的时候到国外旅游。	More and more people like to go on a trip overseas on vacation.
他每天上班以前先去健身房運動。 他每天上班以前先去健身房运动。	Every day he goes to work out in a gym before going to work.
我剛來這家公司上班，想多交幾個新朋友。 我刚来这家公司上班，想多交几个新朋友。	I just started working in this company; I'd like to make some new friends.

包 *bāo*, Another Useful Phonetic

You learned, in Character Writing Workbook 1, about the usefulness of the two components of most Chinese characters: radicals and phonetics. Radicals help you to understand the generic meaning of a character, and phonetics can assist with approximating pronunciation. Radicals and phonetics, meaning and sound, are both 'friends' of the learner of Chinese. Among the 7,000 commonly used characters, fully 80% are composed of one part radical and one part phonetic, and in most of those, the radical is on the left and the phonetic is on the right. Nice and regular, for the most part, and good for us learners who are looking for any help we can get.

In Unit 4 of Character Writing Workbook 1, you learned how useful these five phonetics were:

馬/马	青	門/门	巴	分

Without fretting over tones, can you pronounce all of them? Can you recall any characters that are phonetically associated with them? Work with a partner; share your results with others.

Here's another useful phonetic. 包 (*bāo*) links phonetically to:

雹	*báo*	'hailstones'	with the 雨 ('rain') radical
飽/饱	*bǎo*	'have eaten one's fill'	with the 食/饣 ('food, eat') radical
刨	*bào*	'a plane' (carpenter's tool)	with the 刀 ('knife') radical
抱	*bào*	'hug; embrace'	with the 手 ('hand') radical
鮑/鲍	*bào*	'abalone'	with the 魚/鱼 ('fish') radical

Now phonetics, like radicals, are not always fully reliable. Sometimes they appear as a 'near phonetic.' 包 (*bāo*) is one of these, showing up sometimes as *pao. Bao, bao, bao = pao*! Examples:

跑	*pǎo*	'to run; go about doing something'	with the 足 ('foot') radical
炮	*pào*	'firecracker'	with the 火 ('fire') radical
泡	*pào*	'bubbles'	with the 水 ('water') radical

We understand that many of the characters listed above are brand new, and you likely will not learn them until later in your Chinese career. However, we urge you to become increasingly acquainted with useful phonetics even at this early stage of your learning process. We promise—no, guarantee!—substantial rewards.

打 (dǎ)

dǎ	Later Form	Modern Form
beat; play; make; do; get; etc. (*depending on the object*)	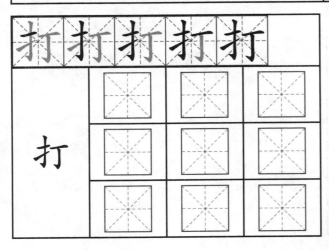	打
dǎqiú		打球

The original meaning of 打 was 'to hit or to strike.' 手/扌 on the left is the radical indicating the whole character is related to hand or hand action. 丁 (*dīng*) on the right is the phonetic component, although only the initial consonant *d* is reliable. 打 is used very widely in modern Chinese. Depending on the objects that follow, 打 has as many as 23 different meanings in any given modern Chinese dictionary. Some of these meanings are related to hand action; others are not. Here are a few examples that are easy to remember.

打氣/打气	'pump up; encourage'	打工	'do part-time work; do odd jobs'
打電話/打电话	'give someone a call'	打的 (*dǎdī*)	'take a taxi'
打聽/打听	'pry into; ask about'	打字	'type; typewrite'
打太極拳/打太极拳	'do *taijiquan*'	打球	'play a ball game'

中國人喜歡打太極拳，也喜歡打麻將。	中国人喜欢打太极拳，也喜欢打麻将。
我給老王打了一個電話，向他打聽一下他那個城市裡有哪些好飯館。	我给老王打了一个电话，向他打听一下他那个城市里有哪些好饭馆。
用手寫漢字很麻煩，我喜歡用電腦打字。	用手写汉字很麻烦，我喜欢用电脑打字。
你週末來和我們一起打籃球吧。	你周末来和我们一起打篮球吧。

球 (*qiú*)

qiú	Later Form	Modern Form
ball; anything shaped like a ball	球	球
dǎ lánqiú		打籃球／打篮球

The original meaning of 球 was 'fine jade ball.' Later 球 was used to mean 'ball' and 'anything shaped like a ball.' 球 is formed with two parts. 王 (*wáng*) on the left is the radical, meaning 玉 (*yù*, 'jade'). 求 (*qiú*) on the right is the phonetic component. Note that when 王 stands alone, it means 'king' and is pronounced *wáng*. When 王 is used as a radical, it is usually a radical meaning 'jade.' For example, we have learned the characters 玩 (originally meaning 'to play with jade'), 理 (originally meaning to 'organize jade'), and 現／现 (originally meaning 'to expose jade; to appear'). 球 appears in compound words relating to 'ball,' 'ball game,' or 'ball shaped.' For example:

地球 land + ball = 'earth'	球門／球门 ball game + gate = 'goal' (in a ball game)
足球 foot + ball = 'soccer'	網球／网球 net + ball = 'tennis'

我哥哥打籃球打得很好。	我哥哥打篮球打得很好。
你玩足球，網球，還是羽毛球？	你玩足球，网球，还是羽毛球？
現在地球上的人越來越多了。	现在地球上的人越来越多了。
美國人玩足球可以用手，那叫美式足球。	美国人玩足球可以用手，那叫美式足球。

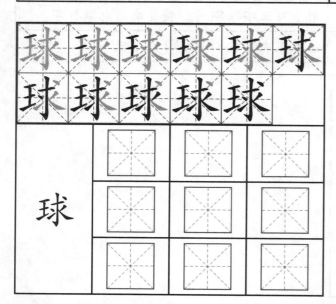

旅 (lǚ)

lǚ	Ancient Form	Later Form	Modern Form
travel; lodge; traveler	![ancient form]	![later form]	旅
lǚyóu			旅遊/旅游

The original meaning of 旅 was 'an army unit on the march.' The ancient form was a sketch of two people marching behind a flag. Later the flag was written as 方 on the left. From the meaning of 'an army on the march,' 旅 was extended to mean 'travel' or 'travel-related things.' When 旅 appears in compound words, it is usually related to 'travel.' For example:

旅客 travel + guest = 'passenger'	旅館/旅馆 travel + accommodation for guests = 'hotel'
旅行 travel + walk = 'travel; journey'	旅遊/旅游 travel + to wander about = 'tour; tourism'

你想到哪個國家旅遊?	你想到哪个国家旅游?
在紐約市('New York City')坐一坐旅遊觀光車很有意思。	在纽约市('New York City')坐一坐旅游观光车很有意思。
美國坐飛機的旅客比坐火車的旅客多。	美国坐飞机的旅客比坐火车的旅客多。
出去旅遊的時候，我都是先打電話訂(dìng, 'to reserve')旅館。	出去旅游的时候，我都是先打电话订(dìng, 'to reserve') 旅馆。

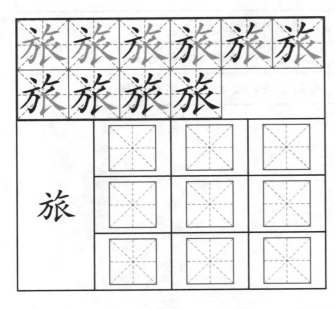

遊/游 (yóu)

yóu	Ancient Form	Later Form	Modern Traditional Form	Modern Simplified Form
swim; travel; wander	𓀀	游	遊	游
lǚyóu			旅遊	旅游

The ancient form of this character is a sketch of a person walking with a flag. So the original meaning of this character was 'streamer; flag.' The ancient form was later written as 斿 and became the right-hand side of 遊/游. 斿 looks very similar to the character 旅 (*lǚ*) we just learned. A streamer flying in the wind looks like a water stream, so 斿 was extended to mean 'wandering in water.' Later this meaning was represented by a new character 游, which was created by adding a 水/氵 radical to 斿. Gradually, 游 was used more often and the character 斿 went out of use. Note that 遊 is a variant of 游, not its traditional form. In the modern traditional character system, 游 is used when the activities are related to water or have water-like quality, and 遊 is used when the activities are related to walking or playing. In the modern simplified character system, however, 遊 has been dropped, and 游 is used for all kinds of activities. 遊/游 appears in compound words relating to 'swim,' 'travel,' or 'wander.' For example:

游泳 swim + swim = 'swim'	旅遊/旅游 travel + wander = 'travel'
遊戲/游戏 wander + game = 'game'	遊客/游客 travel +guest = 'tourist'

每年美國哪個城市的遊客最多？	每年美国哪个城市的游客最多？
你游泳游得快不快？	你游泳游得快不快？
現在的小孩子都喜歡玩電子遊戲。	现在的小孩子都喜欢玩电子游戏。
我們家每年都要到外國去旅遊。	我们家每年都要到外国去旅游。

Modern Traditional Form	Modern Simplified Form
遊 遊 遊 遊 遊 遊	游 游 游 游 游 游
遊 遊 遊 遊 遊 遊	游 游 游 游 游 游
遊	游

聽/听 *(tīng)*

tīng	Ancient Form	Later Form	Modern Traditional Form	Modern Simplified Form
listen; obey			聽	听
tīng yīnyùe			聽音樂	听音乐

The ancient form of this character was formed with an ear next to two mouths, representing the meaning of 'to listen.' It was later extended to mean 'to obey.' Gradually, two characters, 听 and 聽, were created and used at different times in history. Now, the modern traditional character system uses 聽, whereas the modern simplified character system uses 听. 听 has the radical 口 (*kǒu*, 'mouth') on the left. The right part of 听 is 斤. 斤 is the phonetic component and another radical because 斤 is the left part of the character 欣 (*xīn*), meaning 'happy.' 听 originally meant 'listen happily.' 聽 is formed with the radical 耳 (*ěr*, 'ear') at the top left, the phonetic component 壬 (*tìng*) at the bottom left, and the right part of 德 (*dé*, 'virtue; moral') on the right. The right part of 聽 here is another signific component indicating that listening is a very important virtue. 聽/听 appears in compound words relating to 'listen' or 'obey. ' For example:

聽寫/听写 listen + write = 'dictation'	聽話/听话 listen + words = 'obedient'
聽覺/听觉 listen + sense = 'sense of hearing'	好聽/好听 good + listen = 'pleasing to the ear'

今天中文課的聽寫我沒聽懂，所以寫錯了。	今天中文课的听写我没听懂，所以写错了。
我喜歡聽歌劇，也喜歡聽音樂會。	我喜欢听歌剧，也喜欢听音乐会。
你説什麼？大聲一點，我聽不清楚。	你说什么？大声一点，我听不清楚。
我哥哥唱歌很好聽。	我哥哥唱歌很好听。

Modern Traditional Form	Modern Simplified Form
聽 聽 聽 聽 聽 聽	听 听 听 听 听 听
聽 聽 聽 聽 聽 聽	听
聽 聽 聽 聽 聽 聽	
聽 聽 聽 聽	
聽	听

音 (yīn)

yīn	Later Form	Modern Form
sound; voice	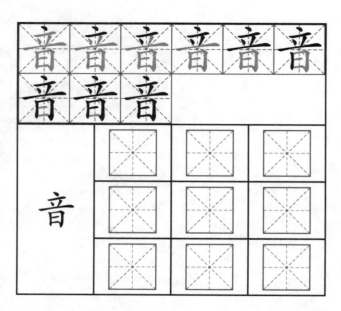	音
yīnyùe		音樂/音乐

Does 音 remind you of the character 言 (*yán*, 'talk')? 言 and 音 were interchangeable in ancient times because both meant the voice or sound from the mouth. Later, 言 was used to mean 'talking; speech,' and 音 was used to mean 'any sound or voice from the mouth.' 言 has 口 (*kǒu*, 'mouth') at the bottom. To differentiate from 言, 音 has 日 (*rì*, 'sun') at the bottom, adding a horizontal stroke inside 口. Gradually, 音 came to be used to mean all kinds of sounds and tones. For example:

音高 sound + high = 'pitch'	口音 mouth + voice = 'accent'
回音 back + sound = 'echo'	音色 sound + color = 'timbre; tone color'

聽你的口音，你是北京人吧？	听你的口音，你是北京人吧？
這個房子很大，在裡面説話都有回音。	这个房子很大，在里面说话都有回音。
我知道你會玩很多樂器，你最喜歡哪種樂器的音色？	我知道你会玩很多乐器，你最喜欢哪种乐器的音色？
你常常聽音樂會嗎？	你常常听音乐会吗？

唱 (chàng)

chàng	Later Form	Modern Form
sing	唱	唱
chànggē		唱歌

唱 is a picto-phonetic character meaning 'to sing.' 口 (kǒu, 'mouth'), on the left, is the radical, indicating the whole character is related to mouth. 昌 (chāng), on the right, is the phonetic component. As your Chinese advances, you will learn more characters with 昌 as the phonetic component.

他每個週末都跟朋友出去喝酒、吃飯、唱歌。	他每个周末都跟朋友出去喝酒、吃饭、唱歌。
唱卡拉OK是從日本開始的。	唱卡拉OK是从日本开始的。
你说中文说得很好，你也會唱中文歌嗎？	你说中文说得很好，你也会唱中文歌吗？
他喜歡玩樂器，也喜歡唱歌。	他喜欢玩乐器，也喜欢唱歌。

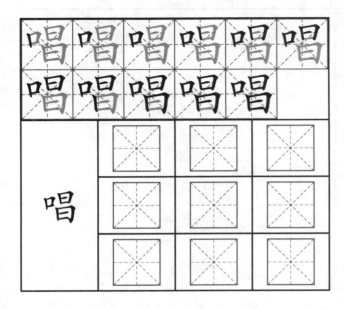

歌 (gē)

gē	Later Form	Modern Form
song; sing	謌	歌
gējù		歌劇/歌剧

The left part of 歌 is the phonetic component. You can see it as two 可 (kě, 'yes'), or you can see it as 哥 (gē, 'older brother'). The right part is 欠, which in the later form is a sketch of a person blowing air (as if playing a musical instrument). 歌 originally meant 'to sing with music.' As you've just learned, 唱 also means 'to sing.' However, 唱 means 'to sing without music.' In modern Chinese, 唱 and 歌 both mean 'to sing,' either with or without music. One major difference between 唱 and 歌 is that 唱 is a verb, while 歌 is mainly used as a noun. You'll only see 歌 used as a verb when it's in compound words. This brings us to another important feature of 歌: 歌 as a verb can't stand alone; it only appears in compound words relating to 'sing' or 'song.' For example:

歌聲/歌声 sing + voice = 'singing voice'	歌劇/歌剧 sing + drama = 'opera'
國歌/国歌 nation + song = 'national anthem'	歌星 sing + star = 'singing star'

他們一家人都愛聽歌劇。	他们一家人都爱听歌剧。
你最喜歡哪個歌星？	你最喜欢哪个歌星？
我覺得你的歌聲非常好聽。	我觉得你的歌声非常好听。

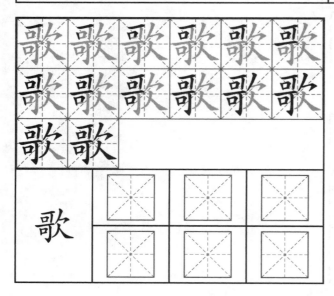

shū	Ancient Form	Later Form	Modern Traditional Form	Modern Simplified Form
book; write			書	书
túshūguǎn			圖書館	图书馆

The original meaning of 書/书 was 'to write.' The ancient form is a sketch of a hand (at the top right) getting a brush (in the middle) out of an inkwell (at the bottom), representing the meaning 'to write.' In the later form, can you still find a hand (at the top) holding a brush (in the middle) and an inkwell (at the bottom)? The modern simplified form is the contour of the modern traditional form in cursive writing. From the meaning 'to write,' 書/书 is extended to mean the result of writing—'books.' In modern Chinese, 書/书 means 'book' when it stands alone and 'to write' or 'book' when it appears in compound words. For example:

書寫/书写 write + write = 'to write'	書法/书法 write + method = 'calligraphy'
書包/书包 book + bag = 'schoolbag'	書店/书店 book + store = 'bookstore'

我們學校的圖書館裡有很多學習中文的書。	我们学校的图书馆里有很多学习中文的书。
我想學習中國書法。	我想学习中国书法。
請問，哪裡有書店？	请问，哪里有书店？
我給小弟弟買的生日禮物是一個新書包。	我给小弟弟买的生日礼物是一个新书包。

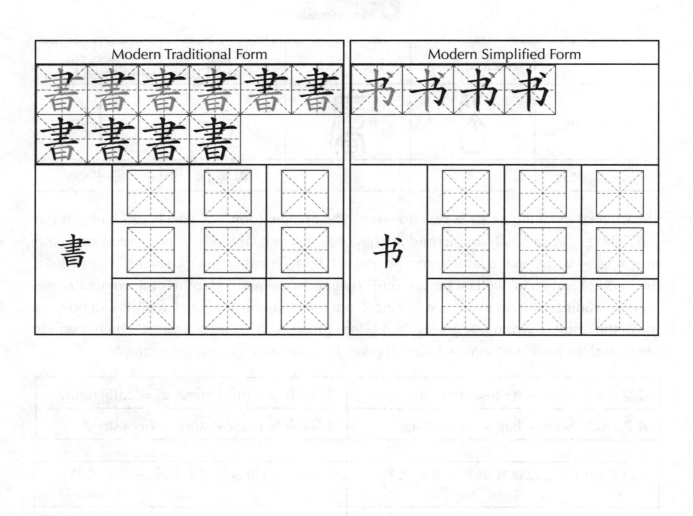

Modern Traditional Form						Modern Simplified Form			
書	書	書	書	書	書	书	书	书	书
書	書	書	書						

書					书			

　Copyright © 2012 by Yale University and China International Publishing Group

gōng	Ancient Form	Later Form	Modern Form
labor; worker; work	𠁁	工	工
gōngzuò			工作

The original meaning of 工 was 'tool.' The form of 工, especially the ancient form, looks like a blade with a handle. A worker needs tools to be more productive, so 工 was later extended to mean 'worker' and 'work.' The original meaning of 'tool' was then dropped. 工 is sometimes used as a phonetic component in compound characters, such as in the character 紅/红 (*hóng*, 'red'). 工 appears in compound words relating to 'work.' For example:

工錢/工钱 work + money = 'wages; pay'	工地 work + land = construction site'
工人 work + person = 'worker; labor'	手工 hand + work = 'handicrafts'

這個工作不忙，可是工錢不多。	这个工作不忙，可是工钱不多。
你喜歡做手工嗎？	你喜欢做手工吗？
你長大以後想做什麼工作？	你长大以后想做什么工作？
老王不在這裡，你到工地上去找他吧。	老王不在这里，你到工地上去找他吧。

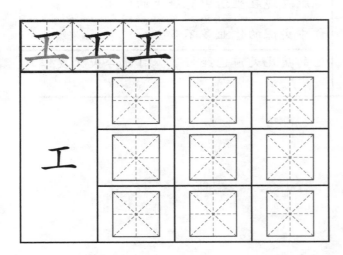

作 (*zuò*)

zuò	Ancient Form	Later Form	Modern Form
rise; make; do			作
zuò zuòyè			做作業/做作业

The original meaning of 作 was 'to get up; to rise.' Some say the ancient form was a sketch of a person sitting up. One gets up because one has something to do. Therefore, 作 was extended to mean 'to make,' 'to do.' In the later form, 亻, 'the standing person' radical, was added to the left. 乍 (*zhà*) on the right is the phonetic component, although it is not very reliable. Compound characters with 乍 are usually pronounced with the initial consonant of either *z* or *zh*. We have learned 昨 (*zuó*, as in 昨天), 怎 (*zěn*, as in 怎麼/怎么), and 炸 (*zhá*, as in 炸雞/炸鸡). You may have noticed there are two different *zuo*s, 作 and 做. As you've learned, both mean 'to do; to make.' So what's the difference? The main difference is that 做 is a verb, and 作 is both a verb and a noun. 作, as a verb, is used mostly to describe academic or intellectual work, as in 作文 ('write an essay') or 作曲 ('write music'). 做, on the other hand, is more about physical or manual work, as in 做工 ('do labor work') and 做晚飯/做晚饭 ('make dinner'). 作 appears in compound words relating to 'do,' 'rise,' or 'work.' For example:

寫作/写作 write + do = 'compose'	作用 do + use = 'function; effect'
作業/作业 do + course of study = 'homework'	發作/发作 start off; occur + rise = 'break out; show effect'

為什麼你週末還要去工作?	为什么你周末还要去工作?
電腦在現在生活中有很大的作用。	电脑在现在生活中有很大的作用。
你中文課的作業多不多?	你中文课的作业多不多?
他的病幾天前已經好了，可是今天又發作了。	他的病几天前已经好了，可是今天又发作了。

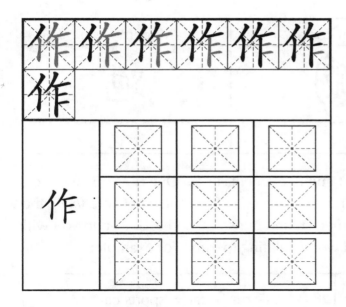

pǎo	Later Form	Modern Form
run; run away	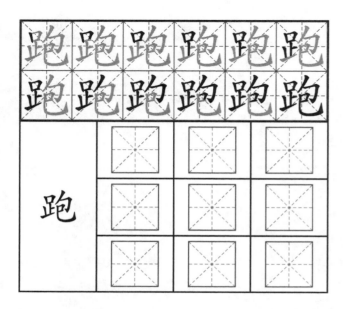	跑
pǎobù		跑步

跑 is a picto-phonetic character. You see two familiar elements in 跑. One is 足 (*zú*, 'foot') on the left, the radical, indicating the whole character is related to foot. The other is 包 (*bāo*), the phonetic component. Remember 包子, steamed stuffed buns? Eat some 包子, and you will be able to run fast. 跑 appears in compound words relating to 'run.' For example:

長跑/长跑 long + run = 'long-distance running'	跑車/跑车 run + car = 'sports car'
跑道 run + road = 'running track'	跑步 run + step = 'running; jogging'

你喜歡在健身房裡跑步還是在外面跑步？	你喜欢在健身房里跑步还是在外面跑步？
他真喜歡運動，天氣那麼冷還出去長跑。	他真喜欢运动，天气那么冷还出去长跑。
快跑吧，要下雨了。	快跑吧，要下雨了。
我們學校的運動場有很多跑道。	我们学校的运动场有很多跑道。

步 (bù)

bù	Ancient Form	Later Form	Modern Form
walk; step	𣥂	𣥂	步
pǎobù			跑步

The original meaning of 步 was 'to walk.' The character form, especially the ancient form, was a sketch of two feet apart, indicating the simultaneous moving of the two feet—walking. Later 步 was extended to mean 'step.' Take a close look at the modern form, and you'll see that the bottom part is very similar to another character you've learned: 少. In modern Chinese, when 步 stands alone, it is a noun, meaning 'step.' When 步 appears in compound words, it means 'to walk' or 'step,' 'pace.' For example:

進步/进步 move forward + step = 'progress'	步入 walk + enter = 'walk into'
同步 same + step = 'synchronous'	讓步/让步 give in + step = 'yield'

我每天下午散步，週末的時候到健身房跑步。	我每天下午散步，周末的时候到健身房跑步。
我覺得你的中文有很大進步。	我觉得你的中文有很大进步。
你的漢字學習要和你的中文學習同步。	你的汉字学习要和你的中文学习同步。
我想他沒有朋友是因為他從來不知道讓步。	我想他没有朋友是因为他从来不知道让步。

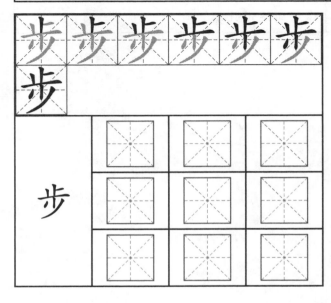

運/运 (*yùn*)

yùn	Later Form	Modern Traditional Form	Modern Simplified Form
move; revolve; transport	連	運	运
yùndòng		運動	运动

運/运 has 辵/辶 ('foot on road') on the left as a radical, indicating the whole character is related to 'walking' or 'moving.' The original meaning of 運/运 was 'military march.' The later form and modern traditional form have 軍/军 (*jūn,* 'army') as the phonetic component and another signific component. The modern simplified form uses 云 (*yún,* 'cloud') as the phonetic component. 運/运 appears in compound words relating to 'move,' 'revolve,' or 'transport.' For example:

運動/运动 move + act = 'exercise'	空運/空运 sky + transport = 'air transport; air freight'
運河/运河 transport + river = 'canal'	運用/运用 move + use = 'utilize; put to use'

你想寄(*jì,* 'send')東西，用空運最快。	你想寄(*jì,* 'send')东西，用空运最快。
在學校學到的東西，要在生活中學習運用。	在学校学到的东西，要在生活中学习运用。
這條運河上每天都有很多運東西的船。 (*chuán,* 'ship, boat')	这条运河上每天都有很多运东西的船。 (*chuán,* 'ship, boat')
你每週運動幾次？	你每周运动几次？

Modern Traditional Form	Modern Simplified Form
運 運 運 運 運 運 運 運 運 運 運 運 運	运 运 运 运 运 运 运

運				运			

動/动 (dòng)

dòng	Later Form	Modern Traditional Form	Modern Simplified Form
move; act	勭	動	动
yùndòng		運動	运动

The original meaning of 動/动 was 'starting to act, to work.' Now it is extended to mean any movement or act. 力 (lì, 'a plough to work on farmland; strength; force') is the radical. The later form and modern traditional form both have 重 (zhòng, 'heavy') as the phonetic component, which you can also consider as a signific component, since a plough is heavy to work with. The modern simplified form dropped the phonetic component 重 and replaced it with 云 (yún, 'cloud'). 云 is not the phonetic component, but we can consider it as another signific component. Isn't a cloud always moving? Be careful to distinguish 动 from 运; both have the same 云 component. 動/动 appears in compound words relating to 'move' or 'act.' For example:

感動/感动 feel + act = 'touch emotionally'	電動/电动 electricity + move = 'electric; power-driven'
自動/自动 self + act = 'automatic'	動聽/动听 move + listen = 'interesting or pleasant to listen to'

現在在北京，很多人騎電動自行車。	现在在北京，很多人骑电动自行车。
這部電影讓我很感動。	这部电影让我很感动。
他的歌聲很動聽。	他的歌声很动听。
你喜歡做什麼運動？	你喜欢做什么运动？

Modern Traditional Form	Modern Simplified Form
動 動 動 動 動 動 動 動 動 動 動	动 动 动 动 动 动

動				动			

約 / 约 (*yuē*)

yuē	Later Form	Modern Traditional Form	Modern Simplified Form
make an appointment; agreement; restriction	約	約	约
yuē péngyou wán		約朋友玩	约朋友玩

The original meaning of 約/约 was 'to bundle up; to bind.' So it has 糸/糸/纟 ('silk') on the left as the radical. 勺, on the right, used to be the phonetic component, but it's no longer reliable. From the meaning of 'bundle up; to bind,' 約/约 was extended to mean 'restriction' and 'agreement,' because 'restriction' and 'agreement' are 'being bundled up abstractly.' When 約/约 appears in compound words, it's usually related to 'agreement.' For example:

約會/约会 agreement + meeting = 'appointment; date'	約見/约见 agreement + see = 'arrange an interview'
約定/约定 agreement + fixed = 'promise'	特約/特约 special + agreement = 'special arrangement'

你週末常常約朋友玩嗎？	你周末常常约朋友玩吗？
對不起，我明天晚上有一個約會，沒空和你去看電影。	对不起，我明天晚上有一个约会，没空和你去看电影。
他們兩個在網上認識幾天後，就互相約見。	他们两个在网上认识几天后，就互相约见。
我們約好這個週末一起去逛博物館，別忘了我們的約定。	我们约好这个周末一起去逛博物馆，别忘了我们的约定。

Modern Traditional Form	Modern Simplified Form
約 約 約 約 約 約 約 約 約	约 约 约 约 约 约

約				约		

交 (*jiāo*)

jiāo	Ancient Form	Later Form	Modern Form
cross; exchange; associate with; join			交
jiāo péngyou			交朋友

Both the ancient and later forms of 交 depict a sketch of a person with legs crossed, indicating the meaning of 'cross' or 'intersect.' Later, 交 was extended to mean 'to exchange,' 'to join,' 'to be associated with.' 交 is a very common phonetic and a pretty reliable one as well. Can you guess the meanings of the following characters, based on the radicals? Look them up in a dictionary to find out the answers. 較, 絞, 郊, 校, 鉸, 餃, 佼, 姣, 跤, 茭, 咬. 交 is used in many compound words. For example:

交談 / 交谈 exchange + talk = 'to converse'	交情 exchange + affection = 'friendship'
交心 exchange + heart = 'bare one's heart; open one's mind'	交通 cross + through = 'traffic'

我和他認識的時間很長，但是沒什麼交情。	我和他认识的时间很长，但是没什么交情。
那次交談以後，我更喜歡這個孩子了。	那次交谈以后，我更喜欢这个孩子了。
你有幾個可以交心的朋友？	你有几个可以交心的朋友？
北京的交通很不好。	北京的交通很不好。

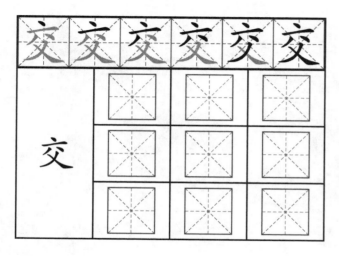

放 (fàng)

fàng	Later Form	Modern Form
release; free; place	放	放
fàngxué		放學 / 放学

放 is a picto-phonetic character. 方 (*fāng*), on the left, is the phonetic component, and 攴/攵 ('action'), on the right, is the radical. 放 usually means 'to release' or 'to free' when it appears in compound words. 放 means 'to put,' 'to place' when it stands alone. For example:

放生 release + life = 'free captive animals'	開放 / 开放 open + to free = 'lift a ban; open to the outside'
放心 to free + heart = 'feel relieved; be at ease'	放大 release + big = 'enlarge; magnify'

美國的小學生每天幾點上學，幾點放學？	美国的小学生每天几点上学，几点放学？
媽媽看到我回來後，才放心地去睡覺了。	妈妈看到我回来后，才放心地去睡觉了。
中國開放以前，很少有外國人到中國。	中国开放以前，很少有外国人到中国。
這個字我看不清楚怎麼寫，請你把字放大一點。	这个字我看不清楚怎么写，请你把字放大一点。

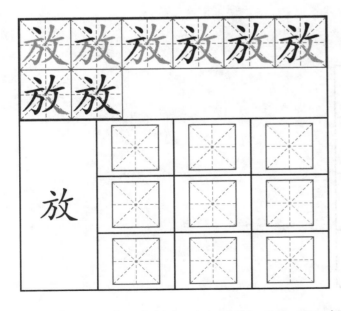

wài	Later Form	Modern Form
out; outside; foreign; alien	朴	外
wàimian		外面

外 has the radical 夕 (*xī*) on the left, which means 'evening.' 卜 (*bǔ*, a pictographic character, a crack on a tortoise shell) on the right means 'divination.' Usually, divination should be done during daytime. 外 depicts a divination done in the evening, indicating an important foreign war affair. Therefore, 外 is used to mean 'out,' 'outside,' 'alien.' For example:

外語/外语 outside + language = 'foreign language'	外衣 outside + clothes = 'coat'
外地 beyond + land = 'parts of the country other than where one is'	外交 alien + exchange = 'diplomacy; foreign affairs'

你會說幾門外語?	你会说几门外语?
他不是去外國工作，他是去外地工作。	他不是去外国工作，他是去外地工作。
你可以把你的外衣放在這裡。	你可以把你的外衣放在这里。
我長大後想做外交工作。	我长大后想做外交工作。

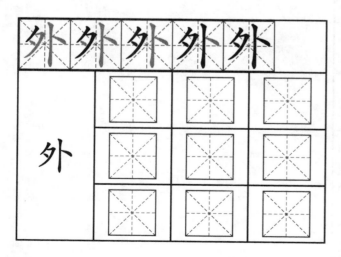

Copyright © 2012 by Yale University and China International Publishing Group

Unit 16

The sentences below are inspired by the contents of Unit 16 and contain all the new characters required for writing as well as others. Read and reread until fluent, covering the English as you read. Then cover the English and try to reproduce the Chinese equivalents orally. Do this exercise before beginning to practice writing.

他帶我們去參觀他的母校。 他带我们去参观他的母校。	He gave us a tour of his alma mater.
我們明天的英語課有一個考試。 我们明天的英语课有一个考试。	Our English class is having an exam tomorrow.
她高中讀的是理科，將來想當個科學家。 她高中读的是理科，将来想当个科学家。	She studies the sciences in senior high school; she wants to become a scientist in the future.
這棟校長辦公樓是去年才完成的。 这栋校长办公楼是去年才完成的。	This president's office building was not finished until last year.
學校的餐廳從早上六點開始賣早餐。 学校的餐厅从早上六点开始卖早餐。	The school cafeteria starts selling breakfast at six o'clock in the morning.
她從初中一直到大學畢業，都是班上第一名。 她从初中一直到大学毕业，都是班上第一名。	From middle school through college graduation, she had the best grades (number one) in her class.
我們學校只有一個圖書館，可是裡面的書又多又新。 我们学校只有一个图书馆，可是里面的书又多又新。	Our school has only one library, but there are a lot of new books in there.
他主修教育，經常有許多課外活動去參觀學校。 他主修教育，经常有许多课外活动去参观学校。	He majors in education; he regularly has lots of extracurricular activities to visit schools.

The Nineteen 'Human' Radicals

In Unit 13 of this book you learned to ask the 'Seven Questions' as a means to locate the position of the radical in a Chinese character. Locating the radical is important for fluent use of a Chinese dictionary, but associating the radical with the meaning of the character is vital to success in reading comprehension. Here are some radicals that are all related to the subject of our common humanity, with character-examples of each in both traditional and simplified forms where applicable. Most of them you've seen before, but perhaps there are one or two new ones. Can you link the meaning of the radical to the meanings of the character-examples?

Body	尸	屋
Child	子	孩 學/学
Ear	耳	聊
Eye	目	看 睡 眼
Flesh/Moon*	月	朋 有 服
Food	食/饣	餓/饿 飯/饭 飽/饱
Foot	足	跟 路 跑
Hand	手/扌	打 把 找 拿
Heart	心/忄	意 思 怎 念 您 想 忘 忙 怕 情 快 慢
Illness	疒	病 瘦
King	王	王 玉 全 現/现
Mouth	口	吃 嗎/吗 吧 問/问 喝 味 唱 叫
Person	人/亻	他 你 位 住 個/个 合 會/会 做 們/们
See	見/见	覺/觉 視/视 觀/观
Son	兒/儿	兒 儿 兄 先
Speech/Word	言/讠	說/说 話/话 請/请 談/谈 課/课 讀/读 謝/谢 語/语
Walk	走/辶	道 近 邊/边 進/进 遠/远
Walking	行/彳	行 很 街 得 往
Woman	女	好 媽/妈 她 姐 妹 姓 始

---

*As we have learned in Unit 12, 月 represents two radicals, 'moon' and 'flesh/meat.'

校 (*xiào*)

xiào	Later Form	Modern Form
school	栲	校
xuéxiào		學校/学校

The original meaning of 校 was a type of instrument of torture. 木 (*mù*, 'wood'), on the left, is the radical, indicating 校 is made of wood. 交 (*jiāo*, 'cross, join'), on the right, is the phonetic component and also a signific component because a 校 was used to bound a criminal's feet together so he or she couldn't walk freely. As the 校 was used to punish and educate criminals, the meaning of 校 was later extended to 'educate; check; proofread,' with the pronunciation *jiào*, or 'a place for educating or civilizing,' with the pronunciation *xiào*. *Xiào*'s original meaning is now obsolete. Here are some examples of 校 used in compound words:

校對/校对 (*jiàoduì*) check + correct = 'proofread'	校花 school + flower = 'the prettiest female student'
校友 school + friend = 'alumnus; alumna'	母校 mother + school = 'alma mater'

我們學校有一個校長，三個副校長。	我们学校有一个校长，三个副校长。
我和小王是校友。她是我們這個年級的校花。	我和小王是校友。她是我们这个年级的校花。
你有沒有再回母校看看？	你有没有再回母校看看？
這本書已經寫完了，正在校對中。	这本书已经写完了，正在校对中。

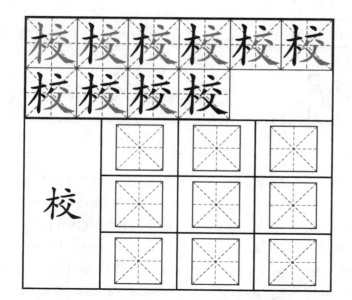

jiāo / jiào	Ancient Form	Later Form	Modern Form
teach; educate	執	敎	教
jiāo wàiyǔ			教外語/教外语
jiàoyù			教育

The character 教 reflects the Chinese tradition of teaching. 攴/攵, on the right, looks like a hand holding a whip or stick. On the bottom left is 子 (*zǐ*), meaning 'child.' The two crosses on the top left (changed in the modern form) represent counting. The idea of this character is 'using a strict way to teach kids to learn math.' Later 教 was used to mean 'teach; educate; instruct' in general. Note that when 教 stands alone, it is pronunced with the first tone (*jiāo*). When 教 appears in compound words, it is pronunced with the fourth tone (*jiào*). For example:

教師/教师 teach + master = 'teacher'	教練/教练 teach + practice = 'coach'
教父 religion + father = 'godfather'	道教 morals + religion = 'Taoism'

我們學校的教師都很喜歡這位新校長。	我们学校的教师都很喜欢这位新校长。
他是我的教父，也是我的籃球教練。	他是我的教父，也是我的篮球教练。
她在我們學校的新教學樓裡教建築。	她在我们学校的新教学楼里教建筑。
道教在中國已經有很長的歷史了。	道教在中国已经有很长的历史了。

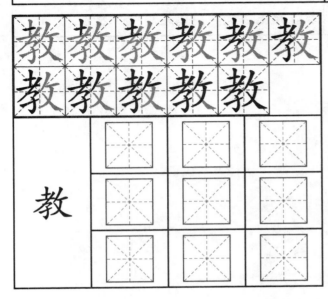

lóu	Later Form	Modern Traditional Form	Modern Simplified Form
a building of two stories or more; a story or floor of a storied building	樓	樓	楼
jiàoxuélóu		教學樓	教学楼

樓/楼 means 'a storied building.' 木 (*mù*, 'wood'), on the left, is the radical, which is easy to understand because old storied buildings were made of wood. 婁/娄 (*lóu*, 'hollow'), on the right, is the phonetic component and another signific component. 婁/娄 is an important phonetic component in many characters. Here is a bonus for you. 摟/搂 (*lǒu*), with 手/扌 (*shǒu*, 'hand') as the radical, means 'cuddle; embrace.' 樓/楼 is also used to refer to stories or floors of a storied building. For example, 第三樓/第三楼 means 'the third floor.' 樓/楼 appears in compound words relating to 'storied building.' For example:

教學樓/教学楼 teach + learn + storied building = 'classroom building'	樓道/楼道 storied building + road = 'passage'
樓上/楼上 storied building + up = 'upstairs'	辦公樓/办公楼 do + public + storied building = 'office building'

我的公寓樓二樓有一個小飯館。	我的公寓楼二楼有一个小饭馆。
不知道為什麼，今天的樓道裡放了很多東西。	不知道为什么，今天的楼道里放了很多东西。
我的辦公室不在這一棟辦公樓。	我的办公室不在这一栋办公楼。
我在樓上睡覺，媽媽在樓下洗衣服。	我在楼上睡觉，妈妈在楼下洗衣服。

Modern Traditional Form	Modern Simplified Form
樓 樓 樓 樓 樓 樓	楼 楼 楼 楼 楼 楼
樓 樓 樓 樓 樓 樓	楼 楼 楼 楼 楼 楼
樓 樓 樓	楼

樓				楼			

圖/图 (*tú*)

tú	Later Form	Modern Traditional Form	Modern Simplified Form
map; picture; drawing; diagram; plan; scheme	圖	圖	图
túshūguǎn		圖書館	图书馆

The original meaning of 圖/图 was 'map.' 囗 (*wéi*, 'enclosure') represents an area, a city, or a country. The inner part of 囗 depicts a sketch of countries and a mountain. Why does the modern simplified form use 冬 (*dōng*, 'winter') inside? We have no answer. The meaning of 圖/图 has been extended to 'plan; scheme.' Think about when you will turn to a map. Maybe when you're planning a trip? Maybe when a general plans a battle? 圖/图 also has the extended meanings of 'picture; drawing; chart; portrait; diagram.' Be careful to distinguish 囗 from 口 (*kǒu*, 'mouth') when you look up radicals in a dictionary. Do you recall the other two characters that use the same 囗 radical: 國/国, 因? Here are examples of 圖/图 in compound words:

地圖/地图 earth; land + drawing = 'map'	圖書館/图书馆 picture + book + a public space = 'library'
意圖/意图 meaning + plan = 'intention'	力圖/力图 effort + plan = 'strive to do one's best'

請看我們學校的地圖，這棟樓是圖書館，這幾棟樓是教學樓。	请看我们学校的地图，这栋楼是图书馆，这几栋楼是教学楼。
你們學校圖書館裡圖書多不多？	你们学校图书馆里图书多不多？
這個孩子每天都早起晚睡，力圖學好每一門課。	这个孩子每天都早起晚睡，力图学好每一门课。
我不懂他這麼做是什麼意圖。	我不懂他这么做是什么意图。

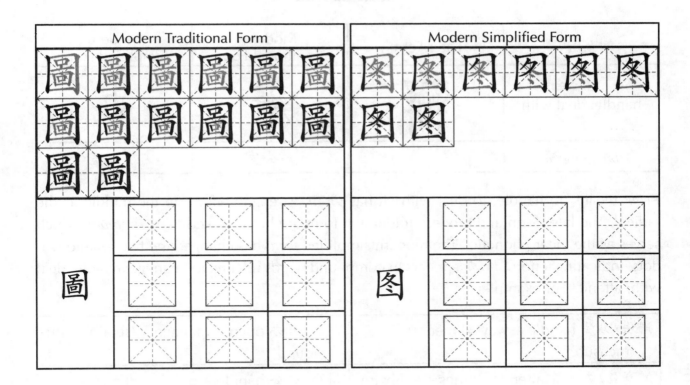

Modern Traditional Form					Modern Simplified Form			
圖					图			

辦/办 (bàn)

bàn	Later Form	Modern Traditional Form	Modern Simplified Form
handle; deal with	辦	辦	办
bàngōngshì		辦公室	办公室

辦/办 means 'to handle, to deal with.' It has 力 (lì, 'strength; effort') in the middle as the radical. The later form and modern traditional form are both flanked with 辛 (biàn), which serves as the 'near phonetic.' The modern simplified form has changed the two 辛 into two dots, indicating 'effort.' 辦/办 appears in compound words relating to 'manage; handle; deal with; attend.' For example:

辦法/办法 handle + way = 'means; measure'	開辦/开办 open + manage = 'set up; start; found'
辦事員/办事员 attend + things + suffix for person = 'clerical personnel'	辦公/办公 handle + public = 'handle official business'

這棟樓是我們學校教師的辦公樓。	这栋楼是我们学校教师的办公楼。
小王是我們辦公室的辦事員。	小王是我们办公室的办事员。
以後我有錢了，我想開辦一個學校。	以后我有钱了，我想开办一个学校。
我的化學總是學不好，你有什麼好辦法？	我的化学总是学不好，你有什么好办法？

Modern Traditional Form	Modern Simplified Form
辨 辨 辨 辨 辨 辨 辨 辨 辨 辨 辨 辨 辨 辨 辨 辨	办 办 办 办

辨			

办			

gōng	Ancient Form	Later Form	Modern Form
public; fairness	公	公	公
xuéshēng gōngyù			學生公寓／学生公寓

八 at the top means 'to divide.' When you divide something, you set the divided parts apart, against each other. So 八 was later extended to mean 'against; opposite.' 口 in the ancient form can mean 'boundaries of a village or tribe' or 'mouth; everyone.' The two parts combined represent the idea of 'dividing food among everyone,' which will require 'fairness.' So, 公 came to mean 'fair; fairness; public.' By the way, characters that have the component 八 (or its inverted form ﹀) usually carry the original meaning of 'division.' Do you recall these characters: 小, 少, 半, 分? 公 appears in compound words relating to 'fair' or 'public.' For example:

公開／公开 public + open = 'make public'	公園／公园 public + garden = 'park'
公車／公车 public + vehicle = 'bus'	公平 fair + flat; level = 'unbiased; fair'

我們學校的學生公寓離教師辦公樓不太遠。	我们学校的学生公寓离教师办公楼不太远。
我家附近有一個很漂亮的公園。	我家附近有一个很漂亮的公园。
他今天公開了他有女朋友的事。	他今天公开了他有女朋友的事。
爸爸總是讓媽媽坐公車上班，自己開車上班，這很不公平。	爸爸总是让妈妈坐公车上班，自己开车上班，这很不公平。

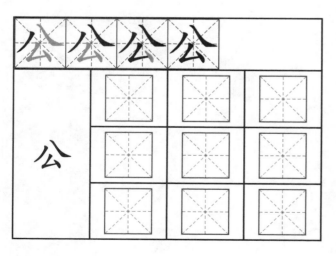

廳/厅 (tīng)

tīng	Later Form	Modern Traditional Form	Modern Simplified Form
hall; main room of a house	廳	廳	厅
cāntīng		餐廳	餐厅

The original meaning of 廳/厅 was 'a hall.' A hall is spacious, so the modern traditional form 廳 has 广 (*guǎng*, 'wall-less hall') and the modern simplified form 厅 has 厂 (*chǎng*, 'wall-less house') as the radical. 廳 uses 聽 as its phonetic component. Remember 聽/听 (*tīng*, 'to listen') from the previous unit? 厅 uses 丁 (*dīng*) as its phonetic component. 廳/厅 appears in a few compound words relating to 'hall' or 'room.' For example:

客廳/客厅 guest + hall = 'reception room; living room'	音樂廳/音乐厅 music + hall = 'concert hall'
舞廳/舞厅 dance + hall = 'ballroom'	餐廳/餐厅 meal + hall = 'cafeteria; restaurant'

我們學校有三個學生餐廳，我常常在第一餐廳吃飯。	我们学校有三个学生餐厅，我常常在第一餐厅吃饭。
我朋友小李每個週末都要去舞廳跳舞。	我朋友小李每个周末都要去舞厅跳舞。
我們學校有一個音樂廳，還有一個電影院。	我们学校有一个音乐厅，还有一个电影院。
客人來我們家的時候，喜歡坐在客廳裡聊天。	客人来我们家的时候，喜欢坐在客厅里聊天。

Modern Traditional Form	Modern Simplified Form

廳 廳 廳 廳 廳 廳
廳 廳 廳 廳 廳 廳
廳 廳 廳 廳 廳 廳
廳 廳 廳 廳 廳 廳
廳

廳

厅 厅 厅 厅

厅

讀/读 (*dú*)

dú	Later Form	Modern Traditional Form	Modern Simplified Form
read; study; attend school	讀	讀	读
dúshū		讀書	读书

We see in 讀/读 the familiar radical 言/讠 (*yán*, 'speech'—the character is a sketch of sound waves above a tongue). 賣/卖 (*mài*, 'to sell'), on the right, is also an old friend we have learned before. 賣/卖 here has nothing to do with trading. It is the phonetic component, although it is not reliable at all. However, it is good to know that characters with 賣/卖 as the phonetic component are pronunced with '*u*' as the final vowel (*dú* here is an example). You will learn these characters when you are at a more advanced level. 讀/读 appears in compound words relating to 'read' or 'study.' For example:

讀音/读音 read + sound = 'pronunciation'	半工半讀/半工半读 half + work + half + study = 'working part time while attending school'
讀者/读者 read + [a suffix meaning someone who does something] = 'reader'	讀後感/读后感 read + behind + feeling = 'post-reading reaction'

我知道這個字的意思，可是我不記得它的讀音了。	我知道这个字的意思，可是我不记得它的读音了。
大學畢業以後，我又半工半讀，讀了一個碩士學位。	大学毕业以后，我又半工半读，读了一个硕士学位。
他想讓一些讀者在讀過他的書以後，寫寫他們的讀後感。	他想让一些读者在读过他的书以后，写写他们的读后感。
你在工作還是在讀書？	你在工作还是在读书？

Modern Traditional Form	Modern Simplified Form
讀 讀	读 读 读 读 读 读 读 读 读 读

讀

读

kè	Later Form	Modern Traditional Form	Modern Simplified Form
class; course (of study)	課	課	课
shàng Zhōngwén kè		上中文課	上中文课

When we have a 課/课, we talk and listen to the teacher and classmates. So it is easy to understand that 課/课 has 言/讠 (*yán*, 'speech') as its radical. 果, on the right, is the phonetic component, although its pronunciation *guǒ* is not relevant to 課/课. 果 means 'fruit; result.' What we care about in a 課/课 is the outcome of what we've learned. Do you agree? 課/课 usually appears in compound words relating to 'class' or 'course.' For example:

課間/课间 class + between = 'recess; break'	副課/副课 secondary + course = 'elective course'
主課/主课 main + course = 'required course'	下課/下课 under; leave + class = 'finish class; dismiss'

你除了上中文課，還上什麼課？	你除了上中文课，还上什么课？
中國中學的課，有主課和副課。	中国中学的课，有主课和副课。
我最好的朋友和我不在同一個班，所以每次課間我都找她玩。	我最好的朋友和我不在同一个班，所以每次课间我都找她玩。
今天我一下課就回家。	今天我一下课就回家。

Modern Traditional Form	Modern Simplified Form
課 課 課 課 課 課 課 課 課 課 課 課 課 課 課	课 课 课 课 课 课 课 课 课 课

課			

课			

考 (kǎo)

kǎo	Ancient Form	Later Form	Modern Form
test; examine; study			考
kǎoshì			考試/考试

考 might remind you of 老 (lǎo, 'old'). If you recall from Unit 11, the ancient form of 考 is the same as the ancient form of 老, an old man with sparse hair and a bent back. 考 and 老 both meant 'old, aged' in ancient times. Later, 考 was borrowed to mean 'examine,' with the bottom changed into the phonetic symbol 丂. In compound words, 考 usually means 'test' or 'study.' For example:

考場/考场 test + field = 'examination hall or room'	高考 high + test = 'entrance examination for college'
考古 study + ancient times = 'engage in archaeological studies'	考生 test + student = 'examinee'

我的中文課每天有一次小考，每週有一次大考。	我的中文课每天有一次小考，每周有一次大考。
今年高考的考生比去年少很多。	今年高考的考生比去年少很多。
這個中學今年也是高考的一個考場。	这个中学今年也是高考的一个考场。
我好朋友的爸爸是考古的，去過很多地方。	我好朋友的爸爸是考古的，去过很多地方。

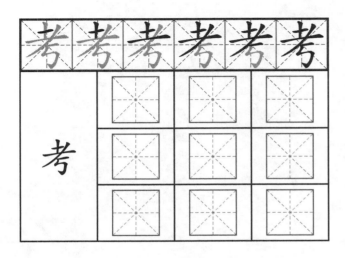

試/试 (shì)

shì	Later Form	Modern Traditional Form	Modern Simplified Form
test; try; examine	試	試	试
kǎoshì		考試	考试

The original meaning of 試/试 was 'to examine a candidate orally before appointing him as a government official.' 言/讠 (*yán*, 'speech'), on the left, is the radical. 式 (*shì*), on the right, is the phonetic component. 式 here is also another signific component because 式 means 'established standard or formula.' Later 試/试 was used to mean 'examine; test.' 試/试 has also been extended to mean 'try; a trial.' For example:

試穿/试穿 try + wear = 'try on a garment or shoes'	試圖/试图 try + plan = 'try; attempt; intend'
口試/口试 mouth + test = 'oral examination'	面試/面试 face + test = 'interview'

我明天中文課有一個大考試，英語課有一個口試。	我明天中文课有一个大考试，英语课有一个口试。
請問，我可以在哪兒試穿這件衣服？	请问，我可以在哪儿试穿这件衣服？
我想主修音樂，可是我媽媽試圖改變我的想法。	我想主修音乐，可是我妈妈试图改变我的想法。
你上個月有過幾個面試，結果怎麼樣？	你上个月有过几个面试，结果怎么样？

Modern Traditional Form	Modern Simplified Form

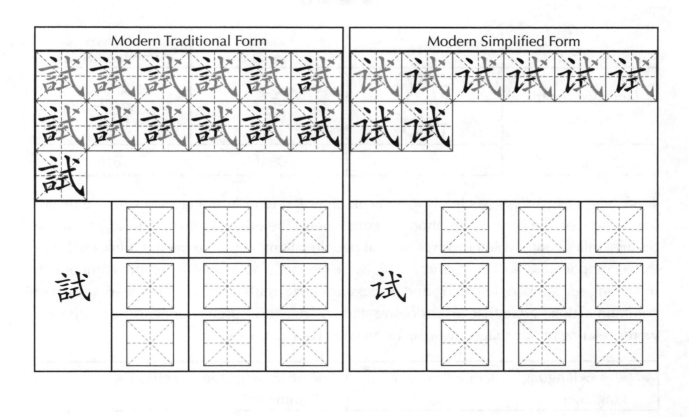

語/语 (yǔ)

yǔ	Later Form	Modern Traditional Form	Modern Simplified Form
language; words; talk	語	語	语
Yīngyǔ		英語	英语

語/语 has 言/讠 (*yán*, 'speech') as its radical. 吾 (*wú*, a term from classical Chinese meaning 'I, me'), on the right, is the phonetic component. The original meaning of 語/语 was 'to discuss; talk about,' which involves several people talking. So some people think 語/语 has three components, 言/讠, 口, and 五. 五 is the phonetic as well as a signific component, indicating several people talking and discussing. 語/语 is also extended to mean 'means of communication.' Note that 語/语 doesn't stand alone. 語/语 usually appears in compound words relating to 'language,' 'words,' or 'to talk.' For example:

語感/语感 language + feel = 'sense of language'	語法/语法 language + method = 'grammar'
手語/手语 hand + talk = 'sign language'	不言不語/不言不语 not + say + not + talk = 'be silent'

他英語學得又快又好，因為他的語感很好。	他英语学得又快又好，因为他的语感很好。
你主修語言學，是研究語法還是語音？	你主修语言学，是研究语法还是语音？
她是不是不高興，怎麼一直不言不語？	她是不是不高兴，怎么一直不言不语？
他遠遠地用手語對女朋友説"我愛你"。	他远远地用手语对女朋友说"我爱你"。

Modern Traditional Form	Modern Simplified Form
語 語 語 語 語 語 語 語 語 語 語 語 語 語	语 语 语 语 语 语 语 语 语

語			

语			

lǐ	Later Form	Modern Form
reason; logic; organize	俚	理
xīnlǐxué		心理學 / 心理学

First, we need to know that when 王 stands alone, it means 'king' and is pronounced *wáng*. But when 王 is a radical in a compound character, it represents 玉 (*yù*, 'jade'). We have learned the character 玩 (*wán*), which originally meant 'to play with jade.' The original character for 'jade' did not have a dot on its right side. Later a dot was added to differentiate it from 'king.' The original meaning of 理 was 'to carve and polish uncut jade.' Therefore, 理 has 王 on the left as the radical, indicating the character is related to 'jade,' and 里 (*lǐ*) on the right as the phonetic component. When you work on uncut jade, you need to observe its internal texture or lines. Therefore, 理 was later used for the abstract concept of 'logic; reason.' 理 has also been extended to mean 'natural science,' since natural science is all about reason and logic. To deal with uncut jade is to deal with all its lines and texture. Therefore, the meaning of 理 has also been extended to 'organize; manage; deal with.' For example:

道理 road; morals + reason = 'principle; reason'	真理 true + logic = 'truth'
管理 control + organize = 'manage; administer'	地理 land; earth + science = 'geography'

我這個學期的課有物理、地理、生物和外語。	我这个学期的课有物理、地理、生物和外语。
我覺得他說的很有道理，我們應該聽他的。	我觉得他说的很有道理，我们应该听他的。
我們家開了一個咖啡館，主要是我媽媽管理。	我们家开了一个咖啡馆，主要是我妈妈管理。
我大學想主修心理學。	我大学想主修心理学。

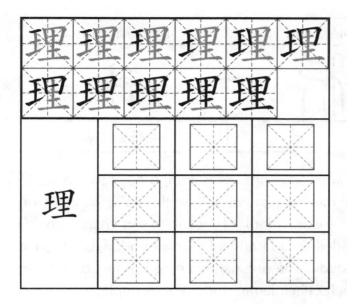

科 (kē)

kē	Later Form	Modern Form
a branch of academic study; a family (of plants or animals)	耤	科
kēxué		科學/科学

The original meaning of 科 was 'to measure and sort grains.' 科 is composed of two radicals. 禾 (hé), on the left, is a pictographic radical meaning 'grains still on the stalk.' 斗 (dǒu), on the right, is a picto-phonetic character of a measuring tool. 科 meant 'to sort grains into different categories,' so its meaning was extended to 'a family (of plants or animals).' Later it also came to mean 'a branch of academic study.' The original meaning is now obsolete. In compound words, 科 usually means 'a branch of academic study.' For example:

醫科/医科 doctor + a branch of academic study = 'medical study in general'	百科全書/百科全书 a hundred + a branch of academic study + whole; entire + book = 'encyclopedia'
眼科 eye + a branch of academic study = 'ophthalmology'	科學/科学 a branch of academic study + study = 'science'

他大學畢業後要學醫科，想做一個眼科醫生。	他大学毕业后要学医科，想做一个眼科医生。
你理科的科目學得好，還是文科的科目學得好？	你理科的科目学得好，还是文科的科目学得好？
電腦科學在我們的生活中越來越重要了。	电脑科学在我们的生活中越来越重要了。
現在在網上也有百科全書。	现在在网上也有百科全书。

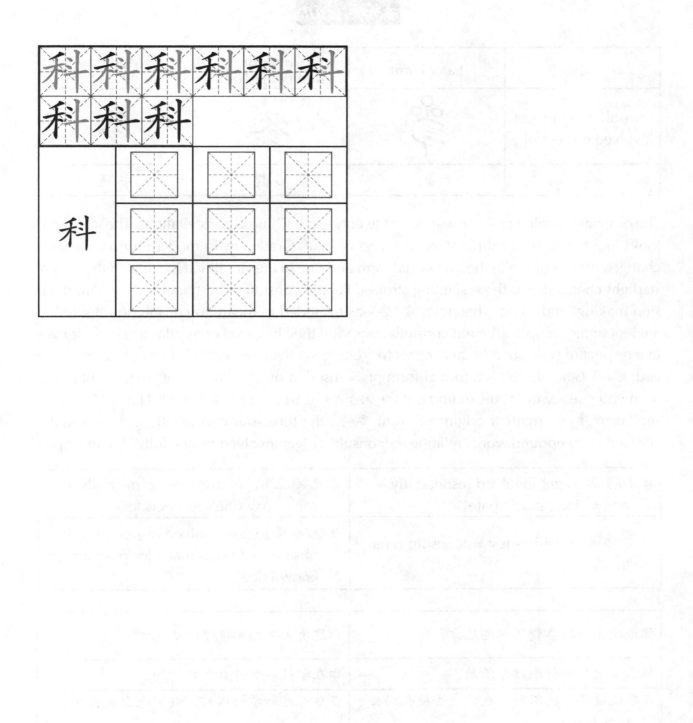

參 / 参 (cān)

cān	Later Form	Modern Traditional Form	Modern Simplified Form
consult, refer to; get involved respectfully		參	参
cānguān		參觀	参观

The original meaning of 參/参 was one of twenty-eight Chinese constellations. The later form looks like a man under three stars with rays of light. Gradually, in modern forms, the stars changed into 厶 (three in the traditional form and one in the simplified form), and the rays of starlight changed into three slanting strokes. People consulted the stars for direction, decision making, and so on. Therefore, 參/参 was extended to mean 'to consult; to refer to.' In ancient times, people admired constellations, and they involved constellations in their lives in a respectful way. So 參/参 also refers to 'getting involved respectfully.' Here is a bonus for you. 叁/叄 (*sān*, 'three') is a formal form of 三, used in official documents to prevent fraud. (Can you guess why? You can find out the answer in Student Book 2, Unit 18.) 叁/叄 is very similar to 參/参, right? It originated from 參/参, the three-star constellation. 參/参 usually appears in compound words relating to 'consult' or 'get involved respectfully.' For example:

參加/参加 to get involved respectfully + add = 'join; participate'	參見/参见 to get involved respectfully + see = 'pay one's respects to'
參考/参考 consult + test = 'consult; refer to'	參觀/参观 to get involved respectfully + observe = 'visit a place for pleasure or knowledge'

你這次去中國參觀了哪些地方？	你这次去中国参观了哪些地方？
你在學校參加什麼課外活動？	你在学校参加什么课外活动？
在參觀這所學校以前，我們先去校長辦公樓參見校長。	在参观这所学校以前，我们先去校长办公楼参见校长。
我要寫我的論文 (*lùnwén*, 'dissertation')，要去圖書館借一些書參考。	我要写我的论文 (*lùnwén*, 'dissertation')，要去图书馆借一些书参考。

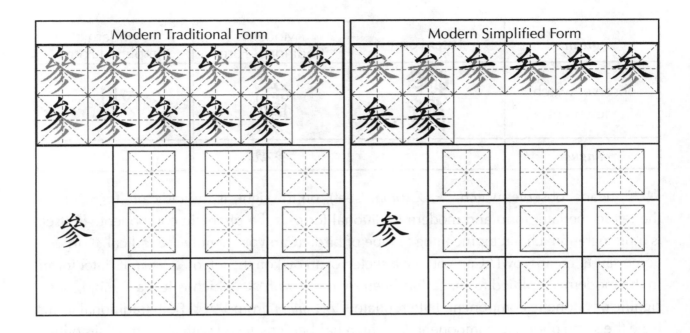

Modern Traditional Form					
参	参	参	参	参	参
参	参	参	参	参	

Modern Simplified Form					
参	参	参	参	参	参
参	参				

参

参

guān	Later Form	Modern Traditional Form	Modern Simplified Form
observe; watch; viewpoint	觀	觀	观
cānguān		參觀	参观

觀/观 means 'observe; watch.' 見/见 (*jiàn*, 'see'), on the right, is the radical. 雚 (*guàn*), on the left in the later form and modern traditional form, is the phonetic component. 雚 itself is a pictographic character meaning 'a type of bird.' (Can you identify the radical 隹 in 雚?) Some say 雚 means 'owl.' Can you see a sketch of an owl on the left of 觀/观 in its later form? In the modern simplified form, 雚 has been replaced with 又, which is just a symbol, not a signific or phonetic component. Differentiate 歡/欢 (*huān*) from 觀/观. Both traditional forms have the same phonetic component 雚, which has been replaced with 又 in both simplified forms. After one observes, one will form a viewpoint or an opinion. So 觀/观 is also used to mean 'viewpoint.' For example:

觀看/观看 to observe + look = 'to gaze; to watch'	美觀/美观 beautiful + watch = 'be pleasing to the eye'
人生觀/人生观 person + life + viewpoint = 'outlook on life'	樂觀/乐观 happy + viewpoint = 'optimism'

我們參觀了很多大學，每個學校的教學樓都很高大、美觀。	我们参观了很多大学，每个学校的教学楼都很高大、美观。
歡迎參觀我的母校，希望你們喜歡我的介紹。	欢迎参观我的母校，希望你们喜欢我的介绍。
他對什麼事情都很樂觀。	他对什么事情都很乐观。
我發現他的人生觀和我的人生觀很不一樣。	我发现他的人生观和我的人生观很不一样。

Modern Traditional Form	Modern Simplified Form
觀 觀 觀 觀 觀 觀	观 观 观 观 观 观
觀 觀 觀 觀 觀 觀	
觀 觀 觀 觀 觀 觀	
觀 觀 觀 觀 觀 觀	
觀	

觀					观			

huó	Later Form	Modern Form
live; survive; active; lively; movable	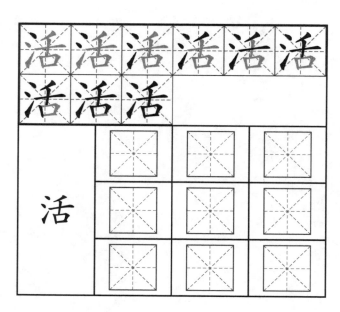	活
huódòng		活動 / 活动

The original meaning of 活 was 'to live; alive.' We see two familiar components in 活: 水/氵 (*shuǐ*, 'water,' a pictographic radical), on the left, and 舌 (*shé*, 'tongue,' a sketch of a tongue sticking out of a mouth), on the right. To live, we need to drink 水/氵, and we need our 舌 to eat. So both 水/氵 and 舌 are radicals. If something is alive, it will be able to move. So 活 is extended to mean 'move; movable; lively.' For example:

生活 birth + live = 'life'	活動 / 活动 move + act = 'activity'
養活 / 养活 support + live = 'raise'	活火山 alive + fire + mountain = 'active volcano'

你參加很多課外活動嗎？	你参加很多课外活动吗？
你最近生活怎麼樣？	你最近生活怎么样？
他一個人上班，養活三個孩子不容易。	他一个人上班，养活三个孩子不容易。
日本有很多活火山，是嗎？	日本有很多活火山，是吗？

完 (wán)

wán	Later Form	Modern Form
whole; complete; finish; be over	宛	完
Chī wán fàn le.		吃完飯了。/吃完饭了。

The original meaning of 完 was 'whole; complete.' It has 元 (*yuán*, 'dollar') on the bottom as the phonetic component. 宀 ('roof'), at the top, is the radical, indicating the character is related to building. The idea is that in ancient times a roof could very easily be blown off or damaged. If the roof was good, then the house could be considered whole or complete. Later, 完 was used as a verb meaning 'finish; complete.' From this meaning, 完 was also used as an adverb meaning 'be over; be through,' as in this sentence: 我讀完大學就開始在這裡工作了。/我读完大学就开始在这里工作了。 In compound words, 完 usually means 'whole; complete,' or 'to finish; to complete.' For example:

完好 whole + good = 'intact, in good condition'	完人 complete + person = 'a perfect man'
完成 finish + succeed = 'accomplish; complete'	完畢／完毕 complete + finish = 'be over; finish'

這棟教學樓是在去年完成的。	这栋教学楼是在去年完成的。
沒有人是完人，但我們都應該試著做一個完人。	没有人是完人，但我们都应该试着做一个完人。
參觀完畢後，我們坐公共汽車回到旅館。	参观完毕后，我们坐公共汽车回到旅馆。
這本書他用了一年，還和新的一樣完好。	这本书他用了一年，还和新的一样完好。

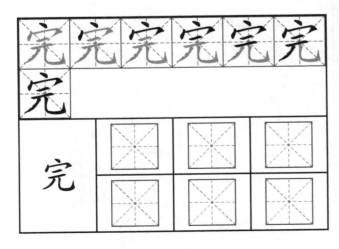

shǐ	Later Form	Modern Form
begin; start	飴	始
kāishǐ		開始／开始

始 means 'begin; start.' 女 (nǔ, 'woman, female'), on the left, is the radical, indicating that we all start being born from a woman. 台 (tái), on the right, used to be the phonetic component, but it isn't any more. 始 appears in a few compound words and many idioms meaning 'begin; start.' Here are two examples:

開始／开始 open + begin = 'begin; start'	始末 begin + end = 'from beginning to end'

你是什麼時候開始學中文的？	你是什么时候开始学中文的？
你明白這件事情的始末嗎？	你明白这件事情的始末吗？

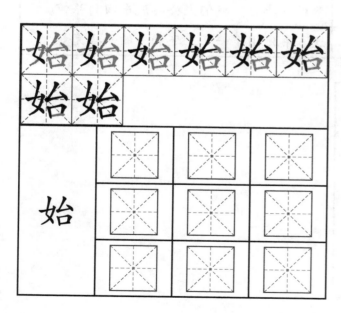

只 *(zhǐ)*

zhǐ	Later Form	Modern Form
only; merely	只	只

只 originally meant 'to sigh helplessly.' It contains a 口 (*kǒu*, 'mouth') and two strokes under 口 like air coming out from sighing. Since the Tang and Song Dynasties, 只 has been borrowed to replace another character, 祇 (*zhǐ*), meaning 'only; merely,' which has the same pronunciation as 只. The original meaning of 只 — 'to sigh helplessly' — was dropped. Nowadays the character 祇 is very rarely used.

Note that in the modern simplified character system, 只 is also used as the simplified form of 隻 (*zhī*). 隻 is a very common measure word for animals, birds, vessels, and one of a pair of things (including hands and feet). That is to say, 只 is doing double duty in the modern simplified character system. Invariably the context of 只 dictates its meaning.

只 is a versatile character. When 只 stands alone, it means 'merely; only.' More often, though, 只 is used in compound words with various meanings. Such adverbs, conjunctions, or verb phrases are very common in daily conversation. For example:

只有 'only, alone; only if'	只好 'can only; have no choice but'
只要 'so long as; if only'	只是 'merely; just; however'

這個周末家裡只有我一個人。	这个周末家里只有我一个人。
我沒有很多錢，我只是一個學生。	我没有很多钱，我只是一个学生。
那個電影，我只看了一半就不想看了。	那个电影，我只看了一半就不想看了。
他沒錢買車，只好做公車上班。	他没钱买车，只好做公车上班。
你只要用心，一定可以學得很好。	你只要用心，一定可以学得很好。

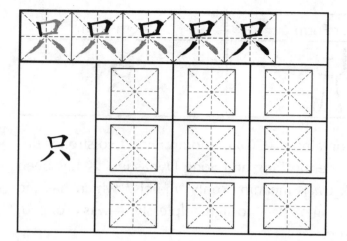

直 (zhí)

zhí	Ancient Form	Later Form	Modern Form
straight; direct; straightforward; continuously	屮	直	直
yìzhí			一直

直 means 'straight.' Do you see an eye (目 *mù*, 'eye') in all the forms of this character? Eyes see straight, so 直 is formed with a vertical line above an eye indicating 'straight.' Gradually the vertical line became 十 (*shí*), which is the phonetic component. The meaning of 直 has been extended to 'direct; straightforward; continuously.' For example:

直觀/直观 direct + view = 'be directly perceived through the senses'	一直 one + continuously = 'continuously; always'
筆直/笔直 pen + straight = 'perfectly straight'	心直口快 heart + straightforward + mouth + quick = 'frank and outspoken'

教孩子學習要用畫圖等很直觀的東西和方法。	教孩子学习要用画图等很直观的东西和方法。
我喜歡和心直口快的人交朋友。	我喜欢和心直口快的人交朋友。
他坐得筆直筆直的。	他坐得笔直笔直的。
我和他一直是很好的朋友。	我和他一直是很好的朋友。

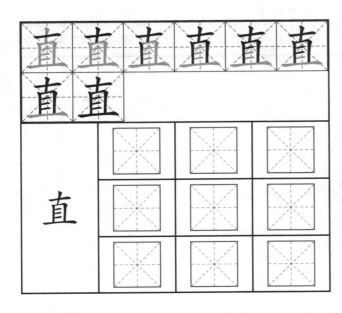

初 (*chū*)

chū	Ancient Form	Later Form	Modern Form
at the beginning; first			初
chūzhōngshēng			初中生

初 means 'at the beginning; in the early part of; first.' It is formed with 衣/衤 (*yī*, 'cloth') on the left and 刀 (*dāo*, 'knife') on the right. The idea is that you start to make clothes by cutting (with 刀) the cloth (衣/衤). Don't confuse the radical 衣/衤 with the radical 示/礻 (*shì*, 'to show'). 礻 has one extra small left-falling stroke that 衤 doesn't have. 衤 appears in compound characters related to cloth. We came across 示/礻 in Unit 13. It often appears in compound characters related to 'religion,' 'ghosts and gods,' 'ancestry,' 'sacrificial rites,' or 'etiquette.' We have learned the following characters that have 示/礻 as a radical: 禮/礼, 祝, 福, 神. 初 appears in compound words related to 'beginning' or 'first.' For example:

年初 year + at the beginning = 'beginning of the year'	初步 first + step = 'initial; first step; tentative'
初試/初试 first + exam; try = 'preliminary examination'	最初 most + at the beginning = 'the very beginning'

我最初想學醫學，後來又想學電腦科學。	我最初想学医学，后来又想学电脑科学。
我初步打算畢業後讀研究生院。	我初步打算毕业后读研究生院。
每年年初，美國各個商場的衣服就賣得便宜很多。	每年年初，美国各个商场的衣服就卖得便宜很多。
在中國，初中讀三年，高中也是讀三年。	在中国，初中读三年，高中也是读三年。

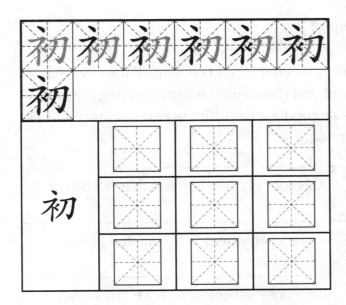

Unit 17

The sentences below are inspired by the contents of Unit 17 and contain all the new characters required for writing as well as others. Read and reread until fluent, covering the English as you read. Then cover the English and try to reproduce the Chinese equivalents orally. Do this exercise before beginning to practice writing.

這個房間很舒服，光線好，又通風。 这个房间很舒服，光线好，又通风。	This room is very comfortable; it's bright and airy.
我們家後院裡種了三棵櫻桃樹。 我们家后院里种了三棵樱桃树。	Three cherry trees were planted in our backyard.
旅館房間裡有自己的衛生間比較方便。 旅馆房间里有自己的卫生间比较方便。	It's more convenient to have one's own bathroom in a hotel room.
我小時候住鄉下，家裡是個平房。 我小时候住乡下，家里是个平房。	When I was little, I lived in a one-story house in the countryside.
她住的公寓裡有兩個臥室，一個客廳。 她住的公寓里有两个卧室，一个客厅。	The apartment she's living in has two bedrooms and one living room.
他記得小時候他家院子裡種了很多花。 他记得小时候他家院子里种了很多花。	He remembers that when he was little, many flowers were planted in the courtyard of his house.
這個房子真大，有兩百個平方米。 这个房子真大，有两百个平方米。	This house is really big—it has two hundred square meters.
我在後院裡種了一些菜，有黃瓜、茄子和 　　西紅柿。 我在后院里种了一些菜，有黄瓜、茄子和 　　西红柿。	I planted some vegetables in the backyard; there are cucumbers, eggplants, and tomatoes.

The Thirty-three 'Nature' Radicals

In Unit 16 we showed you some radicals that were all related in meaning to our common humanity—eye, ear, hand, foot, etc. Listed below are some common radicals that relate to the broad subject of things found in nature. Here's your task: can you link the radical on the left with the meanings of the character-examples on the right? You've seen the characters before, but one or two might be new. Work with a partner or partners.

Bamboo	竹/⺮	等 筷 算
Boundaries	囗	國/国 園/园 圖/图
City/metropolis	阝	都 部 那
Crops/cereals	禾	秋 種/种
Door	門/门	问/問 間/间 閒/闲
Earth/soil	土	坐 地
Family/door	户	房
Fields	田	男 累
Fire	火/灬	點/点 熱/热
Fish	魚/鱼	魚/鱼 鮮/鲜
Food	食/饣	飯/饭 餐 飽/饱
Grass/plants/herbs	艹	草 茶 菜 花
Great/big	大	天
Horse	馬/马	騎/骑
Ice	冫	冰 寒
Knife	刀/刂	別 到 分 剛/刚
Metal	金/钅	錢/钱 鐘/钟
Moon/time	月	期
Mountain	山	出
One/unitary	一	一 七 三 上 下 不 正 百 平 更 事 面
Rain	雨	雷 電/电
Rice	米	粉
Roof	宀	家 室 宿
Shells (for money)	貝/贝	貴/贵 購/购
Silk	糸/纟	紙/纸 結/结

Spacious/space	广	廣/广 店 床 座
Stone	石	碗
Strength/force	力	動/动 助
Sun/time	日	明 早 晚 暖 春 晴 時/时
Tree/wood	木	本 果 樹/树
Water	水/氵	江 河 海 漢/汉 活 洗
Wind	風/风	風/风
Work	工	左 工

房 (*fáng*)

fáng	Later Form	Modern Form
room; house; building	房	房
fángjiān		房間/房间

(For the difference between 房 and 室[*shì*, 'room; bedroom'], please refer to 室 on page 181 of this unit.) 房 is a picto-phonetic character. It originally meant 'side room of a house.' The top part, 户 (*hù*, 'door; family'), is the radical. (Do you see that 户 is a half form of the character 門/门 [*mén*], like a door panel?) 方 (*fāng*) is the phonetic component. Gradually, the meaning of 房 was extended to 'room; house; building.' For example:

房客 room; house + guest = 'tenant (of a room or house)'	廚房/厨房 kitchen + room = 'kitchen'
平房 flat + building = 'single-storied building'	臥房/卧房 recline + room = 'bedroom'

這個平房有三間臥房，這一間光線最好，也最通風。	这个平房有三间卧房，这一间光线最好，也最通风。
這個房子有個很寬敞的廚房。	这个房子有个很宽敞的厨房。
我買了一棟房子，我住一樓，房客住二樓和三樓。	我买了一栋房子，我住一楼，房客住二楼和三楼。
我大學剛剛畢業，沒有錢買房子。	我大学刚刚毕业，没有钱买房子。

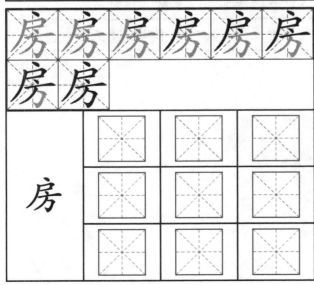

jiān	Later Form	Modern Traditional Form	Modern Simplified Form
gap; space; between	閒	間	间
fángjiān		房間	房间

The later form of 間/间 has 月 inside 門/门. It pictures moonlight shining between the two door panels and indicates 'gap,' 'space,' and 'between.' The same idea would also apply to sunlight, and a new character 間/间 was created, with 日 inside 門/门. 間/间 and 閒 used to be used interchangeably and had the same pronunciation. Later, 閒 (闲 is the simplified form) came to be pronounced *xián* and was used to mean 'not busy; leisure time.' Recall the expression 閒下來的時間/闲下来的时间? A room or a house can be considered as 'a space between walls.' You can often see 間/间 in compound words relating to 'room; house.' 間/间 is also used as a measure word for a room. For example:

中間/中间 center + between = 'among; middle'	課間/课间 class + between = 'break; playtime'
洗手間/洗手间 wash + hand + space = 'lavatory; restroom'	房間/房间 room + space = 'room'

這棟房子有三間臥房，可是只有一個衛生間，不太方便。	这栋房子有三间卧房，可是只有一个卫生间，不太方便。
這個課間我得去洗手間。	这个课间我得去洗手间。
這是我的房間，很寬敞，很舒服。	这是我的房间，很宽敞，很舒服。
我的中文課和物理課中間有十五分鐘。	我的中文课和物理课中间有十五分钟。

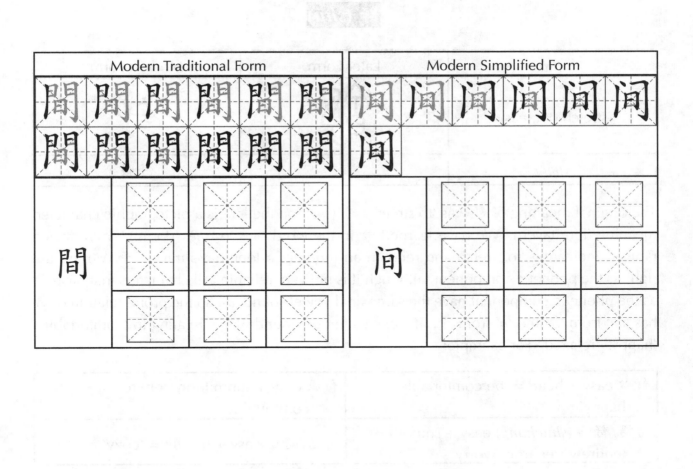

Modern Traditional Form						Modern Simplified Form					
間	間	間	間	間	間	间	间	间	间	间	间
間	間	間	間	間	間	间					

間			

间			

shū	Later Form	Modern Form
stretch out; easy	舒	舒
shūfu		舒服

The original meaning of 舒 was 'to stretch.' 舍 (*shè*), on the left, is a pictographic character, meaning 'inn; tavern.' We have learned 舍 in the word 宿舍 (*sùshè*, 'dorm'). 舍 in 舒 is a radical, indicating 'to stretch and relax in an inn after a long day's travel.' 予 (*yǔ*), on the right, is the phonetic component, although it is not very reliable. All characters that have 予 as the phonetic component have the same final vowel sound '*u*'. So the pronunciation of 舒 has '*sh*' from 舍 and '*u*' from 予. 舒 appears in compound words relating to 'comfortable,' 'happy,' 'relaxed.' For example:

舒心 easy + heart = 'be comfortable/ happy'	舒服 easy + submit (oneself) to = 'comfortable'
舒暢/舒畅 (*shūchàng*) easy + smooth = 'entirely free from worry'	舒適/舒适 easy + fit; suit = 'cozy'

這個音樂聽起來讓人很舒心。	这个音乐听起来让人很舒心。
他說話有時候讓人很不舒服。	他说话有时候让人很不舒服。
我跑完步，洗了澡，全身舒暢。	我跑完步，洗了澡，全身舒畅。
我們住的酒店不大，但讓人覺得很舒適。	我们住的酒店不大，但让人觉得很舒适。

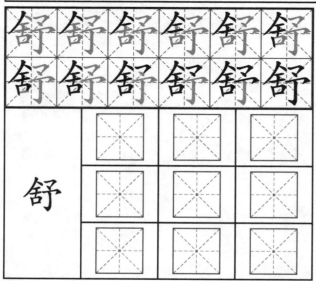

服 (fú)

fú	Ancient Form	Later Form	Modern Form
clothes; obey; surrender; be convinced	服	服	服
shūfu			舒服

The ancient form of 服 is a sketch of a kneeling person controlled by a hand in front of a torture instrument. The original meaning was 'to surrender, to obey.' Who wouldn't surrender under that kind of pressure? The torture instrument on the left somehow became 月 in the modern form. A hand, represented by 又, can still be seen on the right. Is there still a kneeling 人? Yes, if you can see it in the part above 又. 服 is used to mean 'obey; surrender; be convinced.' 服 is also used to mean 'clothes; garments.' Why? Maybe it is derived from wearing things, such as shackles and fetters? For example:

服從/服从 surrender + to follow = 'obey; comply with'	说服/说服 talk + to obey = 'persuade'
工作服 work + clothes = 'work clothes'	心服口服 heart + be convinced + mouth + be convinced = 'be sincerely convinced'

我每天上班都得穿工作服。	我每天上班都得穿工作服。
雖然我不同意他的安排，可是我會服從的。	虽然我不同意他的安排，可是我会服从的。
我說服父母這個週末和我一起去健身房鍛煉。	我说服父母这个周末和我一起去健身房锻炼。
以前沒覺得他籃球打得很好，可是今天跟他打完以後，真是對他心服口服了。	以前没觉得他篮球打得很好，可是今天跟他打完以后，真是对他心服口服了。

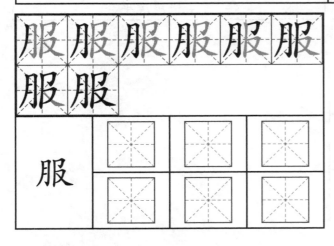

平 (*píng*)

píng	Later Form	Modern Form
flat; equal; even; safe; fair; ordinary	丂	平
píngfāng		平方

The original meaning of 平 was 'gentle; even (in tone).' The bottom part of the later form is a sketch of air being blocked. 八 (*bā*) at the top means 'to divide.' How did that convey the idea of an even and gentle tone? You see, ancient Chinese believed that when one was troubled or upset, one's 氣/气 (*qì*, 'air; energy') would be blocked. When one resolved the troubling or upsetting matter, the air passed through and divided itself evenly, resulting in an even and gentle tone. This concept may be a bit easier to comprehend when you look at the modern form, where the air (the vertical line) actually goes through the horizontal line (the blockage) and then is divided (represented by ᵛ, the inverted form of 八). Later 平 was extended to mean 'flat; equal; even; safe; fair.' From the meaning of 'safe,' 平 was further extended to mean 'ordinary.' For example:

平安 safe + peaceful = 'safe and sound'	平常 safe + invariable = 'usually'
平分 even + to divide = 'divide equally'	平地 flat + ground = 'flat land'
平等 equal + same = 'equality; equal'	公平 just + fair = 'unbiased; fair'

這塊平地上有很多平房，也有幾棟樓房。	这块平地上有很多平房，也有几栋楼房。
我平常六點起床，週末九點起床。	我平常六点起床，周末九点起床。
今天我們做了一樣的工作。可是你分到了八十塊錢，我只分到了二十塊錢，很不公平。這一百塊錢應該平分。	今天我们做了一样的工作。可是你分到了八十块钱，我只分到了二十块钱，很不公平。这一百块钱应该平分。

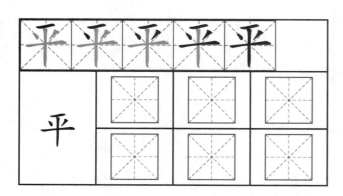

　Copyright © 2012 by Yale University and China International Publishing Group

臥/卧 (wò)

wò	Later Form	Modern Traditional Form	Modern Simplified Form
lie down; sleep	臥 (later form)	臥	卧
wòshì		臥室	卧室

The original meaning of 臥/卧 was 'to lie prone upon.' In ancient times, people would lie prone upon a tea table for a rest when they were tired from reading. The left part of 臥/卧 is 臣—it's a pictographic character—a sketch of an eye looking down. The right part, 人, is a person's profile. The simplified form uses 卜 instead of 人, which adopts as standard a mistake from changes in script style over time. The meaning of 臥/卧 was gradually extended to 'lie down; sleep.' For example:

臥室/卧室 sleep + room = 'bedroom'	坐臥不安/坐卧不安 sitting + lying down + not + peaceful = 'feel restless'
臥遊/卧游 lie down + travel = 'travel vicariously through books and pictures'	臥床不起/卧床不起 lie + bed + not + get up = 'completely bedridden'

這棟房子有三間臥室，一間在一樓，兩間在二樓。	这栋房子有三间卧室，一间在一楼，两间在二楼。
已經晚上十二點了我的孩子還沒回來。我很擔心，真是坐臥不安。	已经晚上十二点了我的孩子还没回来。我很担心，真是坐卧不安。
老王病了，一個月都臥床不起。	老王病了，一个月都卧床不起。
要是你沒錢出門旅遊，在家裡臥遊也挺有意思的。	要是你没钱出门旅游，在家里卧游也挺有意思的。

Modern Traditional Form	Modern Simplified Form
臥 臥 臥 臥 臥 臥 臥 臥	卧 卧 卧 卧 卧 卧 卧 卧

臥			

卧			

shì	Ancient Form	Later Form	Modern Form
room; bedroom			室
jiàoshì			教室

Here's a basic floor plan of a traditional Chinese family home. Inside the main entrance is a hall, called 廳/厅 (*tīng*), which functions as a living room for family gatherings or guests. Behind the 廳/厅 is a 室, which is the bedroom for the most repected people in the family, usually the grandparents or parents. The side rooms next to 室 are called 房 (*fáng*). 房 are usually for concubines. That's why one's second wife is called 二房, the third wife is called 三房, and so on. (Please refer to 房 on page 173 to learn more about that character.) 室 has 宀 ('roof') at the top indicating the whole character is related to house. 至 (*zhì*) is the phonetic component and also another radical. 至 itself is a pictographic character meaning 'to arrive at.' Graphically, 至 is an arrow with a horizontal line under it indicating where the arrow falls. The idea is that when one reaches one's 室, one arrives at a place for rest; there is no need for further walking. 室 usually means 'room' in compound words. Sometimes it means 'family' or 'wife.' For example:

辦公室/办公室 handle + public + room = 'office'	教室 teach + room = 'classroom'
王室 king + family = 'royal family'	家室 home + wife = 'wife; family'

這棟教學樓有三十間教室，還有幾間是辦公室。	这栋教学楼有三十间教室，还有几间是办公室。
很多人對英國王室的生活感興趣。	很多人对英国王室的生活感兴趣。
我還沒有家室，一個人去哪兒工作都可以。	我还没有家室，一个人去哪儿工作都可以。
下課後我要到老師辦公室去問一個問題。	下课后我要到老师办公室去问一个问题。

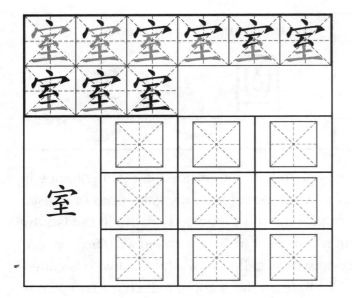

自 (zì)

zì	Ancient Form	Later Form	Modern Form
self	𥄢	𦣞	自
zìjǐ			自己

自 is a pictographic character. It originally meant 'nose,' the sketch of which is especially evident from the ancient form. Now 自 is used in compound words to mean 'self.' Why? Think about the gestures you use when you refer to yourself in talking. Do you point to your nose or around your nose area? From the evolving meanings of 自, we know that ancient Chinese pointed to their noses when they referred to themselves in talking. The original meaning of 'nose' is now represented by a new character, 鼻 (bí), which was created by adding a new phonetic component, 畀 (bì), below 自. 自 means 'self' in most compound words. In a few compound words, 自 also means 'since; from.' For example:

自大 self + big = 'arrogant'	自來水/自来水 self + come + water = 'tap water'
自動/自动 self + move = automatic	來自/来自 come + from = 'from; coming from'

你來自中國什麼地方？	你来自中国什么地方？
他很自大，覺得自己甚麼都比別人好。	他很自大，觉得自己什么都比别人好。
現在很多商店的大門是自動開關的。	现在很多商店的大门是自动开关的。
中國很多地方現在還沒有自來水。	中国很多地方现在还没有自来水。

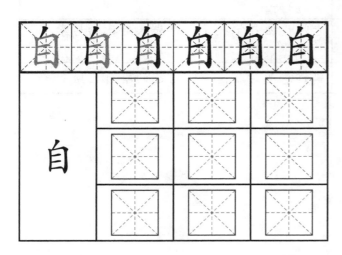

己 (jǐ)

jǐ	Ancient Form	Later Form	Modern Form
oneself	己	己	己
zìjǐ			自己

Originally meaning 'threads in a loom,' 己 depicts the back-and-forth motion of a warp string. 己 meaning 'oneself' is a phonetic loan. Later a new character, 紀/纪 (jì), was created to represent the original meaning by adding the radical 糹/纟 ('silk') to the left. Pay attention to the subtle difference between 己 and 已 (yǐ, 'already'). 己 is a phonetic component in a few characters. For example:

走 ('walking') + 己 = 起 (qǐ, 'rise')	言/讠 ('speech') + 己 = 記/记 (jì, 'write down; mark')
心 ('heart') + 己 = 忌 (jì, 'taboo; fear')	木 ('tree') + 己 = 杞 (qǐ, 'a species of willow')

Note that 自 (zì) and 己 both mean 'self,' but neither of them can stand alone meaning 'self.' For example:

先人後己/先人后己 first + other person + behind + self = 'put others' interests above one's own'	知己 know + self = 'intimate friend; soul mate'

她是我最好的朋友，是我的知己。	她是我最好的朋友，是我的知己。
我現在和朋友一起住，都有自己的臥室和廁所。	我现在和朋友一起住，都有自己的卧室和厕所。
老師說他在學校是一個先人後己的好學生。	老师说他在学校是一个先人后己的好学生。
媽媽總是對我說，"自己的事自己做"。	妈妈总是对我说，"自己的事自己做"。

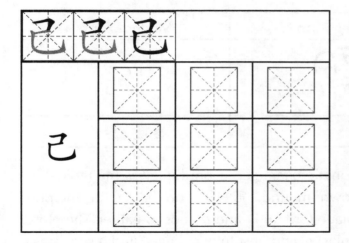

yuàn	Later Form	Modern Form
courtyard; yard	鵤	院
hòuyuàn		後院/后院

院 means 'courtyard; yard.' It is a picto-phonetic character. 阝 on the left is the radical indicating the whole character is related to 'town; mound.' 完 (*wán*), on the right, is the phonetic component. A courtyard is an open place for family and friends to gather. Therefore, the meaning of 院 was extended to 'public places' and 'institute; college,' and it serves as a designation for certain government offices. For example:

後院/后院 behind + yard = 'backyard'	法院 law + government office = 'courthouse'
電影院/电影院 electricity + shadow + public place = 'movie theater'	法學院/法学院 law + study + institute = 'law school'

我們家前院種的有花，後院種的有菜。	我们家前院种的有花，后院种的有菜。
我週六晚上八點在電影院門口等你。	我周六晚上八点在电影院门口等你。
前面那棟很大的樓房就是這個城市的法院。	前面那栋很大的楼房就是这个城市的法院。
他的兒子現在在讀法學院。	他的儿子现在在读法学院。

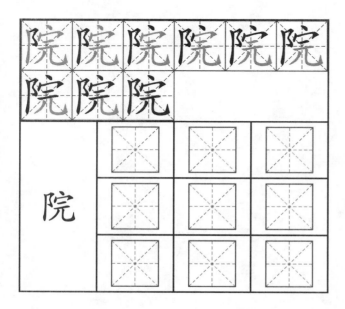

棵 (kē)

kē	Later Form	Modern Form
(measure word for trees, vegetables, etc.)	㮯	棵
yì kē shù		一棵樹／一棵树

棵 is a measure word used mainly for trees and some vegetables such as cabbages and onions. It is a picto-phonetic character. 木 (*mù*, 'tree'), on the left, is the radical. 果 (*guǒ*, 'fruit'), on the right, is the phonetic. *Guǒ > kē*? Not reliable? Remember 課/课 (*kè*, 'class') from Unit 16? When 果 is used as a phonetic component, the whole character has either '*e*' or '*uo*' as final vowels. Or maybe you can consider 果 as another signific component in 棵—a fruit tree, perhaps? 棵 is a measure word, so it doesn't appear in compound words. Below are a few compound characters with 果 as the phonetic component.

衣 (*yī*, 'clothes') + 果 = 裹 (*guǒ*, 'to wrap or bind')	衤 (衣, *yī*, 'clothes') + 果 = 裸 (*luǒ*, 'bare; naked')
頁/页 (*yè*, 'head') + 果 = 顆/颗 (*kē*, 'measure word for a grain-like stuff')	木 (*mù*, 'tree') + 果 = 棵 (*kē*, 'a measure word for trees and some vegetables')
言/讠 (*yán*, 'speech') + 果 = 課/课 (*kè*, 'class')	穴 (*xué*, 'cave') + 果 = 窠 (*kē*, 'a nest; a burrow')

我家後院有三棵蘋果樹。	我家后院有三棵苹果树。
你今天下班回家請幫我買幾棵大白菜。	你今天下班回家请帮我买几棵大白菜。
這棵樹長得很快。	这棵树长得很快。
你知道這是一棵什麼樹？	你知道这是一棵什么树？

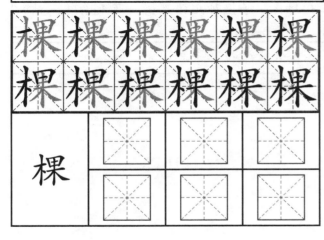

樹/树 (*shù*)

shù	Later Form	Modern Traditional Form	Modern Simplified Form
tree; to plant; erect	𣘗	樹	树
yì kē shù		一棵樹	一棵树

The original meaning of 樹/树 was 'to plant; cultivate.' The later form has a 又 (*yòu*, 'hand') on the right, a 木 (*mù*, 'tree') at the top left, and a 豆 (*dòu*, 'bean') at the bottom left. The three parts together represent the idea of 'a hand holding a tree or a bean plant during planting.' The modern form moves the 木 to the left and uses the standarized form 寸 (*cùn*, 'hand') on the right. Both 木 and 寸 are radicals. The middle part varies in the modern traditional and simplified forms. The traditional form uses 壴 together with 寸 as the phonetic component 尌. Remember the traditional form 廚 (*chú*, 'kitchen')? It also has 尌 as its phonetic component. The simplified form uses 又 ('hand') in the middle as another signific component. From the meaning of 'to plant; cultivate,' the meaning of 樹/树 was later extended to 'tree.' In modern Chinese, 樹/树 means 'to plant; cultivate' only in formal compound words or idioms. For example:

果樹/果树 fruit + tree = 'fruit tree'	樹身/树身 tree + body = 'tree trunk'
樹人/树人 to plant; to cultivate + person = 'nurture men of talent' (formal term)	樹立/树立 to plant + to stand = 'foster; set up' (formal term)

現在中國的城市種了很多樹，越來越漂亮了。	现在中国的城市种了很多树，越来越漂亮了。
這棵樹的樹身已經乾了，看來這棵樹已經死了。	这棵树的树身已经干了，看来这棵树已经死了。
我想在院子裡種幾棵果樹，春天看花，秋天吃果。	我想在院子里种几棵果树，春天看花，秋天吃果。
中國人常常说，十年樹木，百年樹人。	中国人常常说，十年树木，百年树人。

Modern Traditional Form	Modern Simplified Form
樹 樹 樹 樹 樹 樹 樹 樹 樹 樹 樹 樹 樹 樹 樹 樹	树 树 树 树 树 树 树 树 树

樹				树			

種/种 (*zhòng/zhǒng*)

zhòng/zhǒng	Later Form	Modern Traditional Form	Modern Simplified Form
(*zhòng*) plant; grow (*zhǒng*) seed; kind; sort; type	穜	種	种
zhòngshù		種樹	种树

種/种 is a picto-phonetic character. It originally meant 'to sow.' 禾 (*hé*), on the left, is a pictographic character meaning 'grains still on the stalk.' 禾 is the radical. 重 (*zhòng*), on the right, is the phonetic component. The modern simplified form replaces 重 with another phonetic component, 中 (*zhōng*). Do you remember the characters we learned earlier that have 禾 as the radical? Here are two: 香 (Unit 12); 科 (Unit 16). Can you list more?

From the meaning of 'to sow,' 種/种 was extended to mean 'seed,' with the pronunciation of *zhǒng*. From 'seed,' the meaning was further extended to 'kind; sort; type.' In compound words, 種/种 usually means 'kind,' 'type,' 'sort,' or 'seed,' with the pronunciation of *zhǒng*. In a few compound words, 種/种 means 'to grow; plant,' with the pronunciation of *zhòng*. For example:

人種/人种 person + kind = 'race'	各種各樣/各种各样 each + type + each + appearance = 'a great variety of'
種子/种子 seed + (a suffix) = 'seed'	種地/种地 to plant + land = 'cultivate land'

你家院子裡今年種了什麼花?	你家院子里今年种了什么花?
美國可能是不同人種最多的國家。	美国可能是不同人种最多的国家。
我今年想種菜，你能不能給我一些菜種子?	我今年想种菜，你能不能给我一些菜种子?
這個市場上，有各種各樣的水果和蔬菜。	这个市场上，有各种各样的水果和蔬菜。

Modern Traditional Form	Modern Simplified Form
種 種 種 種 種 種 種 種 種 種 種 種 種 種	种 种 种 种 种 种 种 种 种

種			

种			

花 (huā)

huā	Later Form	Modern Form
flower; flowering plant; varicolored; spend	𣎥	花
yǎnghuā		養花 / 养花

花 means 'flower.' The later form of 花 is a pictographic character. It looks like a sketch of a special type of flowering plant. The modern form of 花 is a picto-phonetic character. 艸/艹 (*cǎo*, 'grass'), at the top, is the radical. 化 (*huà*), at the bottom, is the phonetic component. There are many different flowers and colors; therefore, 花 was extended to mean 'varicolored; flower-like pattern.' 花 meaning 'to spend' is a phonetic loan. In compound words, 花 mainly means 'flower,' 'flower-like pattern,' 'to spend,' or 'varicolored.' For example:

花邊/花边 flower-like pattern + edge = 'decorative border; lace'	花錢/花钱 spend + money = 'spend/cost money'
花茶 flower + tea = 'flower-scented tea'	眼花 eye + varicolored = 'have blurred vision'

你這花養得真好，開花的時間也很長。	你这花养得真好，开花的时间也很长。
這件衣服很漂亮，可是我不喜歡衣服上的花邊。	这件衣服很漂亮，可是我不喜欢衣服上的花边。
這家旅館的房間又寬敞又舒服，可是太花錢了。	这家旅馆的房间又宽敞又舒服，可是太花钱了。
看電腦時間太長了你會覺得有點眼花，應該出去走走。	看电脑时间太长了你会觉得有点眼花，应该出去走走。

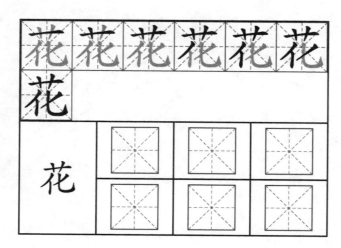

jì	Later Form	Modern Traditional Form	Modern Simplified Form
remember; keep in mind; record	訳	記	记
bǐjì		筆記	笔记

The original meaning of 記/记 was 'to record; write down.' 記/记 is a very straightforward picto-phonetic character. What will one record or write down? Usually it is someone's words, which is 言/讠 (yán, 'speech'). Or think of it this way: if you record or write down something, you need to use a written language. That is 言/讠. So 言/讠 on the left is the radical. 己 (jǐ), on the right, is the phonetic component. We have learned quite a few characters with 言/讠 as the radical. Let's review some of them here. Do you know any more?

請/请	謝/谢	話/话	語/语	談/谈	試/试	讀/读	課/课

Usually one writes down or records something so one won't forget it later. Therefore, the meaning of 記/记 has been extended to 'remember.' 記/记 was then further extended to mean the result of recording or writing, which is a 'note' or 'record (written account).' For example:

記住/记住 to remember + to stay = 'bear in mind; commit to memory'	日記/日记 day + to write down = 'diary'
遊記/游记 travel + note = 'travel notes'	筆記/笔记 pen + note = 'notes'

我可以看看你今天上課的筆記嗎?	我可以看看你今天上课的笔记吗?
他的電話號碼我記不住, 你記住了嗎?	他的电话号码我记不住, 你记住了吗?
我從中學開始寫日記, 一直到今天。	我从中学开始写日记, 一直到今天。
去旅遊的時候, 我每天晚上都寫遊記。	去旅游的时候, 我每天晚上都写游记。

Modern Traditional Form	Modern Simplified Form
記 記 記 記 記 記 記 記 記 記	记 记 记 记 记
記	记

較/较 (*jiào*)

jiào	Later Form	Modern Traditional Form	Modern Simplified Form
compare; contrast; relatively	較	較	较
bǐjiào		比較	比较

較/较 originally meant 'a crossbar on a cart,' which was often decorated. 車/车 (*chē*, 'cart; car') on the left is the radical. In the later form, the part on the right looks like some decoration. In the modern forms, this 'decoration' has become 交 (*jiāo*), which is the phonetic component. In ancient times, the Chinese could tell a person's wealth and social status by the crossbar. Therefore, the meaning of 較/较 was extended to 'compare; contrast; comparatively.' The original meaning is now obsolete.

較/较 appears in only a few very formal compound words and some idioms, so we are not giving examples here. The term we should know now is 比較/比较. Note that 比較/比较 can be a verb meaning 'compare' and an adverb meaning 'fairly; quite; relatively.' In this latter case, 比 can be omitted. For example:

請你比較一下，這兩件衣服，哪件大。	请你比较一下，这两件衣服，哪件大。
這件衣服（比）較大，但顏色不太好看。	这件衣服（比）较大，但颜色不太好看。
你寫的字（比）較大，他寫的字（比）較小。	你写的字（比）较大，他写的字（比）较小。
農村的生活條件（比）較差，城市裡（比）較好。	农村的生活条件（比）较差，城市里（比）较好。

Modern Traditional Form	Modern Simplified Form
較 較 較 較 較 較 較 較 較 較 較 較 較	较 较 较 较 较 较 较 较 较 较

較

较

　　　　Copyright © 2012 by Yale University and China International Publishing Group

衛/卫 (wèi)

wèi	Ancient Form	Later Form	Modern Traditional Form	Modern Simplified Form
guard; protect	衛	衛	衛	卫
wèishēngjiān			衛生間	卫生间

衛/卫 means 'to guard or protect.' In the ancient form, the parts on the left and the right are 'roads extended in all directions,' which is written as 行 in the modern traditional form. 囗 (wéi, 'boundaries'), in the center of the middle part, represents 'city.' Above and below 囗 are 止 (zhǐ, 'foot'). The parts together represent the idea of 'on patrol to guard, to protect.' In the modern traditional form, the middle part becomes 韋 (wéi), which also serves as the phonetic component. Where does the modern simplified form 卫 come from? Some say it is a variant of the middle top part of the modern traditional form. Others say it is from the contour of the cursive writing of the modern traditional form. Anyway, 卫 itself is simple enough to remember. 衛/卫 appears in compound words related to 'guard; protect.' For example:

衛生/卫生 protect + living = 'hygiene; sanitation'	自衛/自卫 self + protect = 'self-defense'
護衛/护卫 defend + to protect = 'guard; protect'	衛星/卫星 guard + star = 'satellite'

你一定要注意衛生，吃東西前要洗手。	你一定要注意卫生，吃东西前要洗手。
你出去旅遊前，應該先學一點自衛方法。	你出去旅游前，应该先学一点自卫方法。
鳥媽媽要一邊護衛自己的孩子，還要一邊找吃的東西。	鸟妈妈要一边护卫自己的孩子，还要一边找吃的东西。
衛星好像是在護衛一個大星星，所以叫衛星。	卫星好像是在护卫一个大星星，所以叫卫星。

Modern Traditional Form	Modern Simplified Form
衛 衛 衛 衛 衛 衛 衛 衛 衛 衛 衛 衛 衛 衛 衛	卫 卫 卫

衛

卫

方 (fāng)

fāng	Ancient Form	Later Form	Modern Form
square; place; direction; way; aspect; side	甹	方	方
píngfāngmǐ			平方米

There are several theories about the origin of this character. Here is the one we think is most reliable. The original meaning of 方 was 'square' or 'parallel.' The ancient form depicts a person (人) carrying a tool (工) to measure and make things square. A square has four sides, so the meaning of 方 was extended to 'side; aspect.' Each side of the square can extend in either direction, so 方 was further extended to mean 'direction.' From 'direction,' the meaning of 方 was yet further extended to 'way; method.' The Chinese in ancient times thought that the sky was dome-like, embracing the vast square earth (天圓地方/天圆地方 *tiānyuán dìfāng*). Therefore, 方 has also been used to indicate the 'earth' and, by extension, 'locality; place; region.' For example:

方言 region + talk = 'dialect'	方法 way + law = 'method; way; means'
東方/东方 east + direction = 'east; the East'	方面 side + face = 'aspect'

你的臥室有多少個平方米?	你的卧室有多少个平方米?
你能聽懂這個地方的方言嗎?	你能听懂这个地方的方言吗?
東方人和西方人在很多方面都很不一樣。	东方人和西方人在很多方面都很不一样。
你覺得有甚麼好方法可以學好中文?	你觉得有什么好方法可以学好中文?

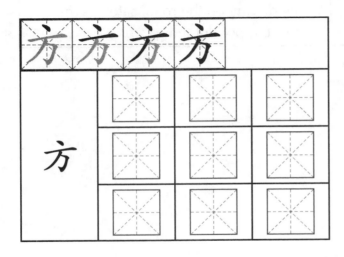

Unit 18

The sentences below are inspired by the contents of Unit 18 and contain all the new characters required for writing as well as others. Read and reread until fluent, covering the English as you read. Then cover the English and try to reproduce the Chinese equivalents orally. Do this exercise before beginning to practice writing.

坐公共汽車雖然慢，可是比較便宜。 坐公共汽车虽然慢，可是比较便宜。	Although taking a bus is time-consuming, it's relatively cheaper.
閒下來的時候，我喜歡打電話和朋友聊天兒。 闲下来的时候，我喜欢打电话和朋友聊天儿。	In my spare time, I like to chat with friends over the phone.
我覺得騎摩托車太危險了。 我觉得骑摩托车太危险了。	I feel that riding a motorcycle is too dangerous.
你如果有公交卡，就不用在車上買票，非常方便。 你如果有公交卡，就不用在车上买票，非常方便。	If you have a public transportation card, you don't have to buy tickets on the bus; it's very convenient.
現在越來越多的人選擇騎自行車上班。 现在越来越多的人选择骑自行车上班。	Nowadays more and more people choose to ride bicycles to work.
行人在大城市過馬路，應該走過街天橋或者地下通道。 行人在大城市过马路，应该走过街天桥或者地下通道。	Pedestrians in big cities should cross the street on a pedestrian overpass or via a pedestrian underpass.
在路上開車，安全最重要。 在路上开车，安全最重要。	While driving on the road, safety is the most important thing.

Fifty Friends for Life: The Most Common Radicals, with Examples

The list below combines the lists of 'Human' radicals and 'Nature' radicals. All fifty of these radicals are worth learning as you continue to study Chinese. And all fifty are shown with character examples that have appeared in the readings. Make a copy of this list and post it prominently in your room. Alternatively, make character flash cards for the radicals and include one or two (or more) examples on each. Review the list and the cards often; we guarantee future benefits.

Ax	斤	斤 新
Bamboo	竹/⺮	等 筷 算 答 簡/简
Body	尸	屋
Boundaries	囗	四 因 回 國/国 圓/园 圖/图
Child	子/孑	孩 學/学
City/Metropolis*	阝	部 那 都
Crops/Cereals	禾	秋 種/种
Door	門/门	門/门 問/问 開/开 間/间 閒/闲
Ear	耳	聊 聞/闻
Earth/Soil	土	在 地 址 坐 城
Eye	目	看 睡 眼 相
Family	戶/户	戶/户 房 所
Fields	田	男 留
Fire	火/灬	點/点 熱/热 炒 然 煮 烤 熟
Flesh/Moon	月	月 朋 有 服 肯 能 望 期
Food	食/饣	飯/饭 餐 飽/饱 餓/饿
Foot	足/⻊	跟 路 跑
Grass/Plants	艹	苦 草 茶 菜 花 英 著
Great/Big	大	大 太 天
Hand	手/扌	手 拿 打 把 找 抄
Heart	心/忄	心 必 意 思 怎 念 您 想 忘 急 忙 怕 情 快 慢
Horse	馬/马	馬/马 騎/骑
Ice	冫	冰 冬 寒 冷 次
Illness	疒	病 瘦 疼
King	王	王 玉 全 玩 球 理 現/现
Knife	刀/刂	別 到 分 剛/刚 前 初

Metal	金/钅	錢/钱　鐘/钟
Mountain	山	山　(歲)/岁
Mouth	口	可　吃　右　只　句　加　合　名　各　員/员　告　嗎/吗　吧　喝　味　唱　叫　和　哪　哥　啊
One/Unitary	一	一　七　三　上　下　不　正　百　平
Person	人/亻	人　他　你　位　住　個/个　但　作　做　們/们
Rain	雨	雨　雷　雪　電/(电)　需
Rice	米	米　粉
Roof	宀	家　室　宿　它　完　安
See	見/见	見/见　覺/觉　視/视　觀/观
Shells	貝/贝	貴/贵　購/购　買/(买)　賣/(卖)　財/财　賺/赚
Silk	糸/纟	紙/纸　經/经　給/给　綠/绿
Son	兒/儿	兒/儿　兄　先　元
Spacious/Space	广	廣/广　店　床　座　店　應/应　底
Speech/Word	言/讠	説/说　話/话　請/请　談/谈　課/课　讀/读　語/语　談/谈　謝/谢　認/认　讓/让　討/讨　論/论　講/讲　許/许　誰/谁
Stone	石	石　碗
Strength/Force	力	力　加　動/动　助
Sun/Time	日	日　明　早　晚　暖　春　晴　時/时　易　是　昨　晨
Terrain/Hill*	阝	陰/阴　陽/阳　除　院　隨/随
Tree/Wood	木	木　樓/楼　東/东　本　果　樹/树
Walk	辵/辶	這/这　道　近　邊/边　進/进　遠/远　過/过　還/还　送
Walking	彳	很　後/(后)　得　往　從/(从)
Water	水/氵	江　河　海　漢/汉　活　洗　沙　汽　法　酒
Woman	女	女　好　媽/妈　她　姐　妹　姓　始　如
Work	工	工　左

* Some Chinese learners call these radicals the 'left and right ears.' When 阝 appears on the right, it relates to 'cities'; when it appears on the left, it relates to 'hills/terrain.'

liáo	Later Form	Modern Form
chat		聊
liáotiān		聊天

聊 is a picto-phonetic character. 耳 (*ěr*, 'ear'), on the left, is the radical. 卯 (*mǎo*), on the right, is the phonetic component. Some scholars consider 卯 to be another signific component because it means 'a mortise' or 'something to secure or fasten two parts'—two people build a connection by chatting (聊). When 聊 stands alone, it means 'chat.' When it appears in compound words, it has different meanings. You will learn them when your Chinese reaches a more advanced level.

我想明天和你聊一聊種樹種花的事。	我想明天和你聊一聊种树种花的事。
在北京坐出租車的時候，我喜歡和司機聊天。	在北京坐出租车的时候，我喜欢和司机聊天。
每星期我都給父母打電話，聊聊學校的事。	每星期我都给父母打电话，聊聊学校的事。
要想學好中文，就應該找機會用中文聊天。	要想学好中文，就应该找机会用中文聊天。

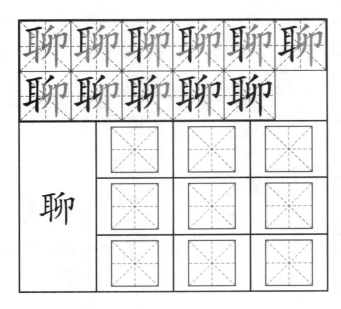

城 (chéng)

chéng	Ancient Form	Later Form	Modern Form
town; city	戌	城	城
chéngshì			城市

城 is a picto-phonetic character. Its original meaning was 'city wall.' It was later extended to mean 'inside the city wall; a town.' 土 (*tǔ*, 'earth, soil'), on the left, is the radical, indicating that the whole character is related to earth and soil. 成 (*chéng*, 'finished'), on the right, is the phonetic and another signific component. 城 in compound words means 'city' or 'town.' For example:

城裡 / 城里 town + inside = 'inside city'	城門 / 城门 city + gate = 'city gate'
城鐵 / 城铁 city + iron = 'city rail'	城市 town + market = 'city'

以前在全中國，城裡城外騎自行車的多極了。	以前在全中国，城里城外骑自行车的多极了。
你知道老北京有幾個城門嗎？	你知道老北京有几个城门吗？
北京和上海這兩個大城市裡有地鐵，也有城鐵。	北京和上海这两个大城市里有地铁，也有城铁。
城鐵在地面上，地鐵在地面下。	城铁在地面上，地铁在地面下。

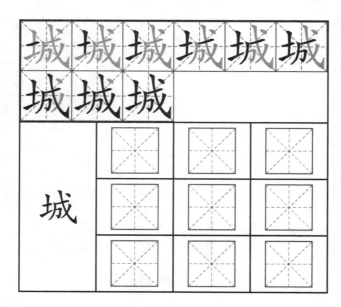

jiē	Later Form	Modern Form
street	街	街
guòjiē tiānqiáo		過街天橋／过街天桥

When you look at 街, you see the character 圭 inside the character 行. 行 (*xíng*) resembles a sketch of roads in different directions, and it means 'road.' 圭 (*guī*) is formed with two 土 (*tǔ*, 'soil, earth') and can be seen as construction work. 街 appears in a few compound words meaning 'street.' For example:

過街天橋／过街天桥 pass + street + sky + bridge = 'pedestrian overpass'	上街 go + street = 'go shopping'
街燈／街灯 street + light = 'streetlight'	街道 street + road = 'street'

在北京過街要走過街天橋。	在北京过街要走过街天桥。
過年的時候，北京街上的街燈很漂亮。	过年的时候，北京街上的街灯很漂亮。
現在買東西都不需要上街了，上網就行了。	现在买东西都不需要上街了，上网就行了。
今天街上人很少，因為天氣不好。	今天街上人很少，因为天气不好。

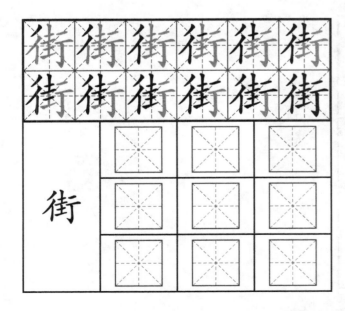

通 (tōng)

tōng	Later Form	Modern Form
through; unimpeded	逋	通
jiāotōng		交通

甬 (*yǒng*), on the right, is the phonetic component. 辵/辶, on the left, is the radical, which indicates 'walking.' If you can walk through something, that means it is 'unimpeded.' Therefore, 通 means 'unimpeded; pass through.' It was later extended to mean 'communicate,' 'traffic,' and 'common.' 通 often appears in compound words related to 'through,' 'communicate,' or 'traffic.' For example:

通過 / 通过 through + pass = 'pass through; by means of'	交通 cross + through = 'traffic'
通知 communicate + know = 'notify'	通用 common + use = 'in common use'

我在北京過馬路的時候，通常走地下通道。	我在北京过马路的时候，通常走地下通道。
通過看電視，他的中文進步了很多。	通过看电视，他的中文进步了很多。
我今天要通知學生，下週五考試。	我今天要通知学生，下周五考试。
美元在世界上是通用的。	美元在世界上是通用的。

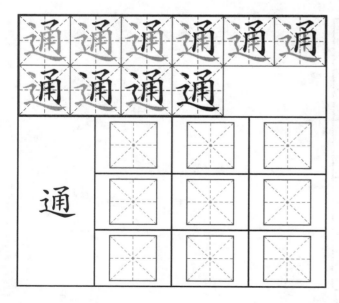

應/应 (yīng)

yīng	Later Form	Modern Traditional Form	Modern Simplified Form
(yīng) should; ought to (yìng) respond	應	應	应
yīnggāi		應該	应该

The original meaning of 應/应 was 'to respond to someone's call or request.' It is pronounced *yìng*. 雁 (*yàn*) is the phonetic component. 心 (*xīn*, 'heart') is the radical, because one should respond to others with heart and sincerity. 應/应 was extended to mean 'should, ought to' with the first tone *yīng*, because once you respond to and agree with others, you should keep your word. 應/应 appears in only a few compound words related to 'should, ought to.' 應/应 often appears in compound words related to 'respond.' For example:

應該/应该 (yīng) should + ought to = 'should; ought to'	應變/应变 (yìng) respond + change = 'respond to an emergency'
答應/答应 (yìng) reply + respond = 'answer; agree'	應時/应时 (yìng) respond + time = 'in season; seasonable'

在大城市，行人從路面上過馬路應該很小心。	在大城市，行人从路面上过马路应该很小心。
我父母答應讓我自己決定畢業後做什麼工作。	我父母答应让我自己决定毕业后做什么工作。
今天在市場上我買了很多應時蔬菜。	今天在市场上我买了很多应时蔬菜。
我覺得我應該提高我的應變能力。	我觉得我应该提高我的应变能力。

Modern Traditional Form	Modern Simplified Form
應 應 應 應 應 應 雁 雁 雁 雁 雁 雁 雁 雁 應 應 應	应 应 应 应 应 应 应
應	应

gāi	Later Form	Modern Traditional Form	Modern Simplified Form
should; ought to		該	该
yīnggāi		應該	应该

The original meaning of 該/该 was 'military obligation.' 言/讠 (yán, 'speech') is the radical (all of the rules are written or spoken for soliders), and 亥 (hài) is the phonetic component. 該/该 is what everyone in an army should obey, and it was later extended to mean 'ought to, should.' The original meaning was abandoned. 該/该 appears in only a few compound words, of which only 應該/应该 ('should; ought to') is used frequently.

請問，到天安門我應該坐地鐵還是坐城鐵？	请问，到天安门我应该坐地铁还是坐城铁？
應不應該買摩托車，你最好問問你父母。	应不应该买摩托车，你最好问问你父母。
你每天都應該吃一些新鮮蔬菜和水果。	你每天都应该吃一些新鲜蔬菜和水果。
我認為她不應該每個週末都逛購物中心。	我认为她不应该每个周末都逛购物中心。

Modern Traditional Form	Modern Simplified Form
該 該 該 該 該 該 該 該 該 該 該 該 該	该 该 该 该 该 该 该 该

橋/桥 (*qiáo*)

qiáo	Later Form	Modern Traditional Form	Modern Simplified Form
bridge	橋	橋	桥
guòjiē tiānqiáo		過街天橋	过街天桥

橋/桥 is a picto-phonetic character. 木 (*mù*, 'wood'), on the left, is the radical, which indicates 橋/桥 is usually made of wood. 喬/乔 (*qiáo*, 'high'), on the right, is the phonetic component and another signific component that indicates 橋/桥 is high above water. Compound words with 橋/桥 usually refer to different kinds of bridges or different parts of a bridge. You will learn them when your Chinese reaches a more advanced level.

要到對面那個購物中心，你應該走過街天橋。	要到对面那个购物中心，你应该走过街天桥。
這條河上有幾座橋？	这条河上有几座桥？
我現在在購物中心前面的過街天橋上等你。	我现在在购物中心前面的过街天桥上等你。
這是一座小石橋。	这是一座小石桥。

Modern Traditional Form	Modern Simplified Form
橋 橋 橋 橋 橋 橋 橋 橋 橋 橋 橋 橋 橋 橋 橋 橋	桥 桥 桥 桥 桥 桥 桥 桥 桥 桥
橋	桥

　　　Copyright © 2012 by Yale University and China International Publishing Group

quán	Later Form	Modern Form
complete; whole; entire	全	全
quánguó		全國 / 全国

全 means 'whole; entire.' The top part is 入 (*rù*, 'enter'). The bottom part, 王, as we have learned before, means 'king' and is pronouned *wáng* when it stands alone. But when it appears in a compound character, it usually means 'jade' and is pronounced *yù*, as is the case here. The two parts together indicate that a jade is complete and perfect. Later it came to mean 'whole' or 'entire.' 全 appears in compound words related to 'entire,' 'complete,' or 'whole.' For example:

全部 entire + part = 'entirely; whole'	安全 quiet + complete = 'safe'
全新 entire + new = 'brand new'	完全 complete + entire = 'complete; completely'

現在城市裡汽車太多，騎自行車有點不安全了。	现在城市里汽车太多，骑自行车有点不安全了。
我爸爸給我買了一輛全新的汽車。	我爸爸给我买了一辆全新的汽车。
今年夏天我要用全部的時間來學習中文。	今年夏天我要用全部的时间来学习中文。
今天這位出租車司機說的話，我完全聽不懂。	今天这位出租车司机说的话，我完全听不懂。

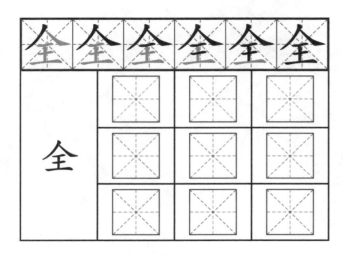

選/选 (xuǎn)

xuǎn	Later Form	Modern Traditional Form	Modern Simplified Form
select; choose	選	選	选
xuǎnzé		選擇	选择

選/选 means 'to select; to choose.' 辵/辶 is the radical, which indicates the whole character is related to 'walking': while walking, one needs to choose a path. The modern traditional form uses 巽 (xùn) as the phonetic component, and the modern simplified form uses 先 (xiān) as the phonetic component. 選/选 appears in compound words related to 'select,' 'choose,' and 'selection.' For example:

選民/选民 select + the people = 'voter'	落選/落选 fall + selection = 'lose an election'
選票/选票 selection + ticket = 'vote; ballot'	選送/选送 select + send = 'select and recommend'

在北京，過街走地下通道是一個安全的選擇。	在北京，过街走地下通道是一个安全的选择。
我們學校每年都要選送最好的學生到外國留學。	我们学校每年都要选送最好的学生到外国留学。
為了得到更多的選票，他常常跟選民聊天，告訴選民他的想法。	为了得到更多的选票，他常常跟选民聊天，告诉选民他的想法。
我覺得這一次他一定會落選。	我觉得这一次他一定会落选。

Modern Traditional Form	Modern Simplified Form

選 選 選 選 選 選
選 選 選 選 選 選
選 選 選 選

选 选 选 选 选 选
选 选 选

選

选

擇/择 (zé)

zé	Later Form	Modern Traditional Form	Modern Simplified Form
pick and choose	擇	擇	择
xuǎnzé		選擇	选择

擇/择 means 'pick and choose.' It involves hand actions, so 擇/择 has 手/扌 (*shǒu*, 'hand') on the left as the radical. The right part of 擇/择 is considered the phonetic component, but it is pronounced *yì* and therefore not helpful here. However, there is a character with 睪 as the phonetic component: 譯/译 (*yì*, 'to translate'). In modern Chinese, 選擇/选择 ('choose; select') is the only compound word.

我們每一次考試都有選擇題。	我们每一次考试都有选择题。
一個是在銀行工作，一個是在學校工作，你會選擇哪一個？	一个是在银行工作，一个是在学校工作，你会选择哪一个？
如果你買禮物給媽媽，這種手機是一個很好的選擇。	如果你买礼物给妈妈，这种手机是一个很好的选择。
你為什麼要選擇在家裡最需要你的時候出去旅遊？	你为什么要选择在家里最需要你的时候出去旅游？

Modern Traditional Form	Modern Simplified Form
擇 擇 擇 擇 擇 擇 擇 擇 擇 擇 擇 擇 擇 擇 擇 擇 擇	择 择 择 择 择 择 择 择

危 *(wēi)*

wēi	Later Form	Modern Form
danger; dangerous	危	危
wēixiǎn		危險 / 危险

危 is an associative character. From the later form, we can see there is 厂 (*chǎng*) in the middle, which represents a cliff. There is a standing person on top of the cliff and a kneeling person below the cliff. The different positions of these two human figures provide a contrast indicating that it is dangerous to stand on a cliff (whereas it's safe to kneel below it). 危 appears in compound words related to 'dangerous.' For example:

危急 dangerous + urgent = 'critical; in imminent danger'	危害 dangerous + impair = 'harm'
病危 sick + dangerous = 'be terminally ill'	人人自危 people + self + dangerous = 'everyone feels insecure'

他弟弟來電話説，爺爺生病了，情況很危急。	他弟弟来电话说，爷爷生病了，情况很危急。
你也覺得騎摩托車很危險嗎？	你也觉得骑摩托车很危险吗？
他爺爺剛剛病危了，所以他很難過。	他爷爷刚刚病危了，所以他很难过。
我們公司有幾個人丢了工作後，現在真是人人自危。	我们公司有几个人丢了工作后，现在真是人人自危。

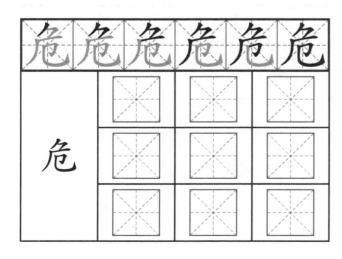

險/险 (xiǎn)

xiǎn	Later Form	Modern Traditional Form	Modern Simplified Form
dangerous; danger	䧫	險	险
wēixiǎn		危險	危险

The original meaning of 險/险 was 'tall and rugged, dangerous terrain.' 阝/阜 (fù, 'hill'), on the left, is the radical, and 僉/佥 (qiān), on the right, is the phonetic component. Recall that the characters 臉/脸 (liǎn, 'face') and 檢/检 (jiǎn, 'check') also have 僉/佥 (qiān) as the phonetic component. 險/险 later came to mean, and be used in compound words that mean, 'risk,' 'dangerous,' or 'difficult.' For example:

脫險/脱险 separate oneself from + risk = 'escape (be out of) danger'	保險/保险 to protect + risk = 'insurance'
山高水險/山高水险 mountain + high + water + dangerous = 'mountains are high, torrents are swift'	千難萬險/千难万险 thousand + difficulty + ten thousand + dangerous = 'very difficult and dangerous'

他告訴我，他爸爸已經脫險了，過幾天就可以從醫院回家了。	他告诉我，他爸爸已经脱险了，过几天就可以从医院回家了。
在美國買車，也要買車保險。	在美国买车，也要买车保险。
從四川到西藏 (Xīzàng—Tibet)，山高水險，開車得很小心。	从四川到西藏 (Xīzàng—Tibet)，山高水险，开车得很小心。
他經過了千難萬險，終於回到了家。	他经过了千难万险，终于回到了家。

Modern Traditional Form	Modern Simplified Form

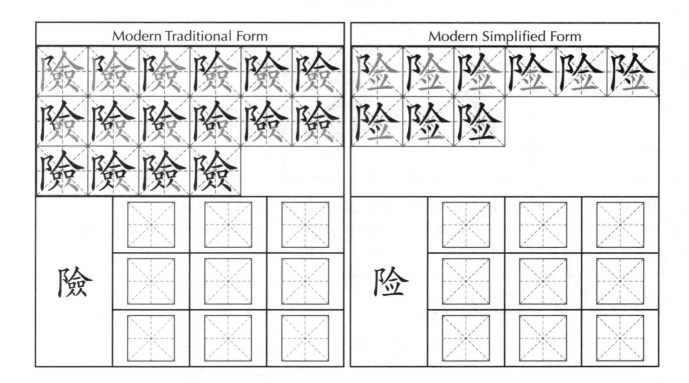

險

险

騎/骑 (*qí*)

qí	Ancient Form	Later Form	Modern Traditional Form	Modern Simplified Form
ride	夨	騎	騎	骑
qímǎ			騎馬	骑马

The original meaning of 騎/骑 was 'to ride a horse.' It is a picto-phonetic character. 馬/马 (*mǎ*, 'horse'), on the left, is the radical, and 奇 (*qí*), on the right, is the phonetic component. Today 騎/骑 is used to mean 'to ride' in general. For example:

騎士/骑士 ride + soldier = 'knight'	騎手/骑手 ride + hand = 'jockey'
騎虎難下/骑虎难下 ride + tiger + difficult + down = 'have no way to back down'	騎馬找馬/骑马找马 ride + horse + look for + horse = 'hold on to one job while seeking a better one'

我想學習了解一下古代騎士的生活。	我想学习了解一下古代骑士的生活。
在大城市騎摩托車和騎自行車一樣危險。	在大城市骑摩托车和骑自行车一样危险。
弟弟說他長大後要當一個好的摩托車騎手。	弟弟说他长大后要当一个好的摩托车骑手。
他發現自己做不好這件事，但已經同意做了，現在真是騎虎難下。	他发现自己做不好这件事，但已经同意做了，现在真是骑虎难下。

Modern Traditional Form	Modern Simplified Form

騎	騎	騎	騎	騎	騎
騎	騎	騎	騎	騎	騎
騎	騎	騎	騎	騎	騎

| 骑 | 骑 | 骑 | 骑 | 骑 |
| 骑 | 骑 | 骑 | 骑 | 骑 |

騎			

骑			

行 (*xíng* / *háng*)

xíng / *háng*	Ancient Form	Later Form	Modern Form
(*xíng*) walk; (*háng*) row; line of business	仆	桃	行
zìxíngchē			自行車 / 自行车

行 can be pronounced *xíng* or *háng*. The original meaning of 行 was 'road,' and the ancient form looks like an intersection of roads. Remember the character 街? Can you find 行 in 街? Roads often look like lines or rows, so 行 is also used to mean 'line' or 'row.' From this meaning, 行 was later extended to mean 'line of business; profession.' For these meanings, 行 is pronounced *háng*. Roads are also for people to walk on, so 行 was later used as the verb 'to walk.' The original meaning of 'road' was dropped. From 'to walk,' 行 gradually came to mean 'to act; to work.' For these meanings, 行 is pronounced *xíng*. 行 appears in compound words related to 'line of business,' 'walk,' or 'do.' For example:

行家 (*háng*) line of business + suffix meaning person = 'expert'	銀行 / 银行 (*háng*) silver + line of business = 'bank'
行為 / 行为 (*xíng*) do + act = 'behavior; action'	人行道 (*xíng*) person + walk + road = 'sidewalk'

他在買車賣車方面是個行家。	他在买车卖车方面是个行家。
你這種行為我不能接受。	你这种行为我不能接受。
他每天騎自行車去銀行上班。	他每天骑自行车去银行上班。
在北京，很多車經過人行橫道的時候，不會慢下來等行人。	在北京，很多车经过人行横道的时候，不会慢下来等行人。

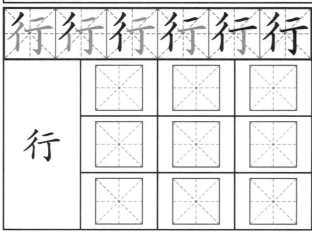

yuè	Later Form	Modern Form
go beyond; skip; more and more (adv.)		越
yuèláiyuè		越來越/越来越

The original meaning of 越 was 'to pass over.' 走 (note the 大 over 止 in the later form) is the radical, which indicates the whole character is related to walking. 戉 (*yuè*) is the phonetic component. 越 was later extended to be an adverb meaning 'much more; further.' In modern Chinese, 越 is usually used in the construction 越來越/越来越 or 越…越…. 越 appears in compound words related to 'to exceed' or 'to skip.' For example:

越級/越级 skip + rank; grade = 'to skip a grade; bypass the immediate leadership'	越禮/越礼 exceed + courtesy = 'not act on etiquette'
越過/越过 exceed + pass = 'cross'	超越 exceed + go beyond = 'exceed; surpass'

越來越多的中國人買了汽車。	越来越多的中国人买了汽车。
天氣越不好，騎自行車的人就越少。	天气越不好，骑自行车的人就越少。
飛機越過城市，越過那條河，很快就看不見了。	飞机越过城市，越过那条河，很快就看不见了。
我希望在中國，很快就會有能超越姚明 (*Yáo Míng*) 的籃球運動員。	我希望在中国，很快就会有能超越姚明 (*Yáo Míng*) 的篮球运动员。

越　越　越　越　越　越
越　越　越　越　越　越

越

共 (gòng)

gòng	Ancient Form	Later Form	Modern Form
common; together	(ancient form)	(later form)	共
gōnggòng qìchē			公共汽車/公共汽车

Graphically, the ancient form of 共 depicts two hands raising a square-shaped item, such as a bowl. 共 originally meant 'to provide; to supply.' It was later extended to mean 'common; together.' From the meaning 'common,' 共 is also used as an abbreviation for the Communist Party of China, as in 中共. The original meaning is now represented by a new character, 供 (*gòng*), which is created by adding a 人/亻 (*rén*, 'person') to 共. 共 is a phonetic component in a few compound characters. For example:

氵(水) + 共 = 洪 (*hóng*) 'floods; turbulent waters'	口 + 共 = 哄 (*hǒng*) 'to cheat; to defraud'
火 + 共 = 烘 (*hōng*) 'to bake; to roast'	共 + 心 = 恭 (*gōng*) 'respectful'

共 appears in compound words related to 'common,' 'share,' and 'together.' For example:

共餐 together + meal = 'have a meal together'	共有 together + have = 'common ownership'
一共 one; whole + together = 'altogether; in all'	公共 public + share = 'public; common'

從這兒到購物中心是坐地鐵方便，還是坐公共汽車方便？	从这儿到购物中心是坐地铁方便，还是坐公共汽车方便？
她喜歡聽他說話，和他共餐。	她喜欢听他说话，和他共餐。
我們宿舍的電視機是我和同學共有的。	我们宿舍的电视机是我和同学共有的。
你知道你一共學了多少個漢字？	你知道你一共学了多少个汉字？

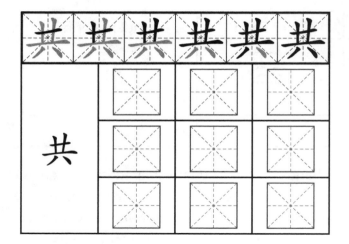

qì	Later Form	Modern Form
steam; vapor	汽	汽
qìchē		汽車/汽车

汽 is a picto-phonetic character. 氵 (水 *shuǐ*, 'water'), on the left, is the radical. 气 (*qì*, 'air,' a pictographic character), on the right, is the phonetic component and another signific component. 汽 appears in compound words related to 'steam' or 'vapor.' For example:

汽車/汽车 steam + vehicle = 'automobile'	汽水 steam + water = 'soda'
汽油 steam + oil = 'gasoline'	水汽 water + vapor = 'water vapor'

我不開車上下班，我坐公共汽車。	我不开车上下班，我坐公共汽车。
小孩子都喜歡喝汽水。	小孩子都喜欢喝汽水。
因為越來越多人買汽車，所以汽油就越來越貴了。	因为越来越多人买汽车，所以汽油就越来越贵了。
空氣中的水汽太多，慢慢地，就會下雨。	空气中的水汽太多，慢慢地，就会下雨。

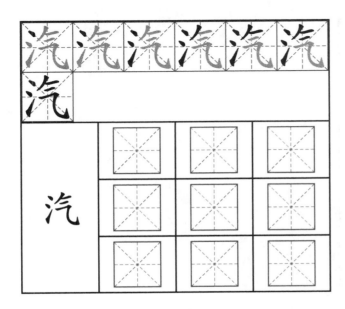

非 (fēi)

fēi	Ancient Form	Later Form	Modern Form
no; not; wrong	飞	非	非
fēicháng			非常

非 is a sketch of a flying bird's two spreading wings. The wings face in opposite directions. Therefore, 非 originally meant 'violate,' 'run counter to,' or 'not conform to.' The opposite of 'right' is 'wrong,' so 非 was extended to mean 'wrong; error.' The opposite of 'yes' is 'no,' so 非 also means 'no; not.' 非 appears in compound words meaning 'not' or 'wrong.' For example:

口是心非 mouth + yes + heart + no = 'duplicity; say yes and mean no'	非法 not + law = 'unlawful'
非常 not + usual = 'unusual; extremely'	是非 right + wrong = 'right and wrong'

我發現他是個口是心非的人。	我发现他是个口是心非的人。
這個孩子還太小，還沒有是非觀念。	这个孩子还太小，还没有是非观念。
你這樣做是非法的。	你这样做是非法的。
今天天氣非常熱。	今天天气非常热。

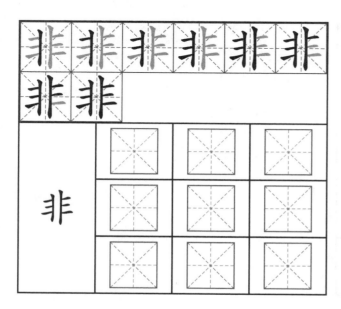

卡 (kǎ)

kǎ	Later Form	Modern Form
card	卡	卡
gōngjiāokǎ		公交卡

卡 is formed with the characters 上 (shàng, 'up') and 下 (xià, 'down'). 卡 is not up, not down, not left, not right. The original meaning of 卡 was a military 'checkpost' or 'checkpoint'—a toll between borders. When you pass a 卡, you need to show some form of an identity certificate or card. Therefore, 卡 was later used for 'card' in general. In compound words, 卡 means 'card.' It is also used as a phonetic transcription for transliteration. For example:

公交卡 public + cross + card = 'transportation (charge) card'	信用卡 honest; sincere + use + card = 'credit card'
卡車/卡车 a phonetic transcription + vehicle = 'truck'	卡通 a phonetic transcription + a phonetic transcription = 'cartoon'

在北京，坐公交車、地鐵、城鐵都能用公交卡。	在北京，坐公交车、地铁、城铁都能用公交卡。
現在越來越多的中國人開始用信用卡了。	现在越来越多的中国人开始用信用卡了。
今年我爸爸想買一輛大卡車。	今年我爸爸想买一辆大卡车。
你喜歡看卡通電影嗎？	你喜欢看卡通电影吗？

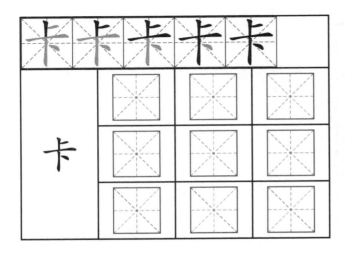

piào	Later Form	Modern Form
ticket	票	票
chēpiào		車票 / 车票

The original meaning of 票 was 'blazing fire.' In the later form, the top part represents two hands holding a torch made of cloth dipped in oil. The bottom part is 火 (*huǒ*, 'fire'), representing 'flames.' The meaning of 票 as 'ticket' is a phonetic loan. Gradually, 'ticket' became its primary meaning, and the original meaning was dropped. The modern form of 票 uses 示 (*shì*, 'show') instead of 火 as the radical. 票 appears in compound words related to 'ticket.' For example:

半票 half + ticket = 'half/reduced fare'	全票 whole + ticket = 'full fare'
門票 / 门票 gate + ticket = 'admission ticket'	月票 month + ticket = 'monthly ticket'

每次坐公共汽車都買票太麻煩，你最好買月票，又方便又便宜。	每次坐公共汽车都买票太麻烦，你最好买月票，又方便又便宜。
北京公交車的票價不太高。	北京公交车的票价不太高。
北京的很多公園都不要門票。	北京的很多公园都不要门票。
小孩子坐火車買半票就可以。	小孩子坐火车买半票就可以。

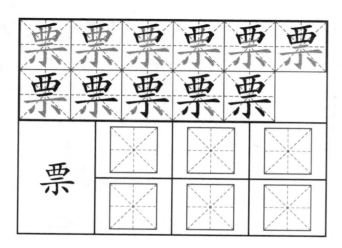

Copyright © 2012 by Yale University and China International Publishing Group

The sentences below are inspired by the contents of Unit 19 and contain all the new characters required for writing as well as others. Read and reread until fluent, covering the English as you read. Then cover the English and try to reproduce the Chinese equivalents orally. Do this exercise before beginning to practice writing.

他決定畢業以後留在國內工作。 他决定毕业以后留在国内工作。	He decided to stay in his home country and work after graduation.
天氣預報說今天會下雨，出門要記得帶把傘。 天气预报说今天会下雨，出门要记得带把傘。	The weather forecast says it'll rain today; remember to bring an umbrella with you when you go out.
春天來了，百花開了，到處都是鳥語花香。 春天来了，百花开了，到处都是鸟语花香。	Spring is here; hundreds of flowers are in bloom. Everywhere one can hear birds chirping and smell the fragrance of flowers.
秋天這裡的樹葉都會變紅，風景非常漂亮。 秋天这里的树叶都会变红，风景非常漂亮。	The leaves here all turn red in the fall; the scenery is very beautiful.
如果明天是晴天，我們就可以去郊外爬山。 如果明天是晴天，我们就可以去郊外爬山。	If it's sunny tomorrow, then we can go hiking in the countryside.
夏天天氣很熱，海灘上太陽很曬。 夏天天气很热，海滩上太阳很晒。	It's hot in the summertime; the sun is very strong on the beach.
去年冬天下了好幾場大雪。 去年冬天下了好几场大雪。	Last winter there were quite a few big snowfalls.

'Alive on Paper': The Art of Chinese Writing

We have reached Unit 19 of our *Encounters* journey. You've come a long way. Our common goal throughout—our principal object—has been to teach you to write Chinese characters properly and accurately. Along the way, we have noted the importance of the connections among writing, recognition, and recall of Chinese characters; that writing reinforces a knowledge of character components; that writing helps you distinguish characters that have a similar shape; and, just as important, that writing is just plain fun. We have not, however, tried to turn you into a calligrapher—a practitioner of fine, beautiful writing—yet it is appropriate, perhaps even obligatory, on our part to share with you some of the tradition of Chinese calligraphy, a tradition that takes writing beyond the practical needs of communication and lifts it to the realm of art.

The Chinese call the art of calligraphy *shūfǎ* 書法/书法 (the way of writing). In China, this art is held in the highest esteem and even surpasses painting and poetry. It has been observed that 'painters are good calligraphers first and good painters second.' The Chinese scholar, the *wénrén* 文人 (man of letters), could, of course, write a fine essay, but unless the calligraphy of that essay was as fine as its content, it was all for naught. Moreover, the appreciation of fine writing was not only the domain of the educated and the rich, it was also claimed by the lesser classes. Even the most common restaurant could be adorned with examples of the calligraphic art, even if not exactly the original.

It is true that the West has its own version of the art of fine writing. However, to the Chinese, Western calligraphy is too mechanical, too lifeless, and too invariable; in a word, it is monotonous. The Western writing style never achieved the level of art that calligraphy has maintained in China for centuries.

What then makes a character beautiful? The key is that characters must be 'alive,' full of movement and life, harmonious, balanced, rhythmic, sometimes gentle and slow, and sometimes swift and bursting with energy—all with the intention of giving inspiration to the viewer and accomplished with seemingly effortless spontaneous motion. Perhaps this sounds like we're overdoing it, but we're not. Unfortunately, only a few people in the West can rise to a true appreciation of Chinese calligraphy. Seeing is believing, however, so get to China; see a calligrapher at work in the studio or even on the street, and you too can get close to the Chinese art of arts.

Two fine books about Chinese writing and calligraphy from which this essay benefited are:

Learn to Write Chinese Characters, Johan Bjorksten (Yale University Press, 1994)

Speaking of Chinese, Raymond Chang and Margaret Scrogin Chang (W. W. Norton and Company, 1978)

The following illustration presents an example of the calligraphic art executed by the twelfth-century Song emperor Huizong.

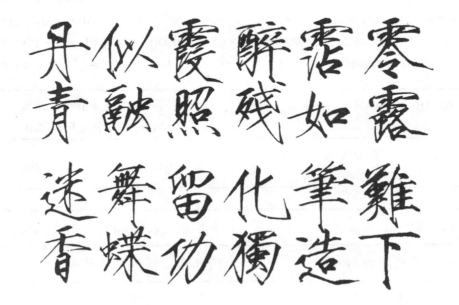

春 (chūn)

chūn	Ancient Form	Later Form	Modern Form
spring			春
chūntiān			春天

The ancient form of 春 is formed with a 日 (*rì*, 'sun'), a little sprout on the right, and two plants, ⺿/艸 (*cǎo*). The sun turns sprouts into plants, which symbolizes that spring is coming. The later form uses 屯 (*tún*) in the middle to represent a sprout. 屯 is also the phonetic component. 春 often appears in compound words related to 'spring.' For example:

春遊／春游 spring + travel = 'spring outing'	春節／春节 spring + festival = 'Chinese New Year; Spring Festival'
春色 spring + color = 'spring scenery; joyful expression'	春季 spring + season = 'spring'

每年春天我都和朋友們去春遊。	每年春天我都和朋友们去春游。
在中國，春節是最熱鬧的節日。	在中国，春节是最热闹的节日。
今年春天來得早，才二月就有了春色。	今年春天来得早，才二月就有了春色。
春季是我最喜歡的季節。	春季是我最喜欢的季节。

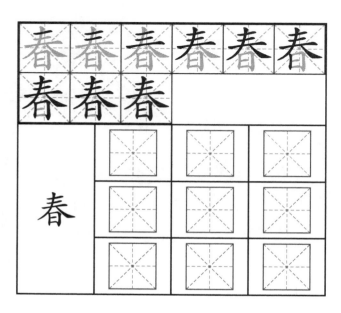

Copyright © 2012 by Yale University and China International Publishing Group

xià	Later Form	Modern Form
summer	夒	夏
xiàtiān		夏天

The later form of 夏 has 頁 (*yè*, 'head') on top, a hanging hand on each side, and a foot at the bottom. Originally, 夏 referred to a group of early Chinese people who lived near the middle and lower reaches of the Yellow River. These people called themselves 夏 to differentiate themselves from nearby minorities. The word 華夏/华夏 (*huáxià*) in modern Chinese still means 'China.' 夏 meaning 'summer' is a phonetic loan. 夏 appears in compound words related to 'summer.' However, with the exception of 夏天 (*xiàtiān*, 'summer') and 夏季 (*xiàjì*, 'summer'), other compound words are rarely used.

住在海邊，夏天的中午很熱，可是早上和晚上很涼快。	住在海边，夏天的中午很热，可是早上和晚上很凉快。
北京的夏天是悉尼 *Xīní* (Sydney) 的冬天。	北京的夏天是悉尼 *Xīní* (Sydney) 的冬天。
一年有四季：春、夏、秋、冬。	一年有四季：春、夏、秋、冬。
夏威夷的夏天舒服極了。	夏威夷的夏天舒服极了。

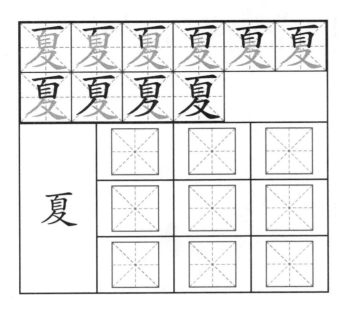

秋 (*qiū*)

qiū	Ancient Form	Later Form	Modern Form
autumn	仌	燩	秋
qiūtiān			秋天

The ancient form of 秋 is a sketch of a cricket. Crickets chirp in autumn, so the ancient Chinese used a drawing of a cricket to represent the season. The later and modern forms use 禾 (*hé*, 'standing grain') and 火 (*huǒ*, 'fire') to symbolize autumn, since grains and leaves all turn red during this time of the year. Some scholars think the 火 in 秋 comes from the seasonal practice of burning straw and stalks left in the field to kill insects. 秋 appears in compound words related to 'autumn,' but only 秋天 (*qiūtiān*, 'autumn') and 秋季 (*qiūjì*, 'autumn') are commonly used.

北京的秋天是最漂亮的時候。	北京的秋天是最漂亮的时候。
北京人在秋天喜歡去爬香山。	北京人在秋天喜欢去爬香山。
一年四季中，我最喜歡秋季。	一年四季中，我最喜欢秋季。
秋天的風景最漂亮，有藍天、白雲、紅葉。	秋天的风景最漂亮，有蓝天、白云、红叶。

秋 秋 秋 秋 秋 秋
秋 秋 秋

秋

Copyright © 2012 by Yale University and China International Publishing Group

冬 (*dōng*)

dōng	Ancient Form	Later Form	Modern Form
winter			冬
dōngtiān			冬天

In ancient times, people kept records by tying knots. The ancient form of 冬 is a sketch of a string with two ending dots, which emphasize 'end.' The original meaning of 冬 is 'end; terminal.' According to the lunar calendar, winter falls in October, November, and December, which is the end of the year. Therefore, 冬 was used to mean 'winter.' The original meaning of 'end; terminal' is today represented by a new character, 終/终 (*zhōng*). In the later form, 仌 was added to represent a sketch of ice piles. 冬 appears in compound words related to 'winter,' but only 冬天 (*dōngtiān*, 'winter') and 冬季 (*dōngjì*, 'winter') are commonly used.

我們這裡的冬天常常下雪。	我们这里的冬天常常下雪。
他喜歡冬天，因為他喜歡滑雪。	他喜欢冬天，因为他喜欢滑雪。
春、夏、秋、冬，四個季節中，你最喜歡哪個？	春、夏、秋、冬，四个季节中，你最喜欢哪个？
冬天這裡的風景也很漂亮。	冬天这里的风景也很漂亮。

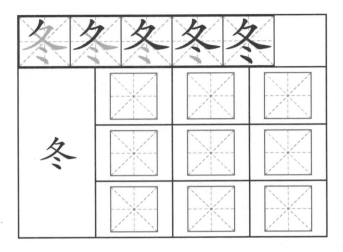

陽/阳 (yáng)

yáng	Ancient Form	Later Form	Modern Traditional Form	Modern Simplified Form
sun	𨸜	陽	陽	阳
shài tàiyáng			曬太陽	晒太阳

The original meaning of 陽/阳 is 'south of a hill.' China is in the northern hemisphere, so the south side of a hill always receives sunshine. Later, 陽/阳 came to mean 'sun.' 阝, on the left, is the radical, which indicates that the whole character is related to 'hill' or 'wall.' 昜 (*yáng*), on the right, is a phonetic component and another signific component because 昜 consists of 日 (*rì*, 'sun') and 彡 ('sunshine'). The modern simplified form of 阳 dropped 彡. 陽/阳 appears in a few compound words related to 'sun.' For example:

陽光/阳光 sun + light = 'sunshine; sunlight'	陽曆/阳历 sun + calendar = 'solar calendar'
太陽/太阳 the greatest + sun = 'sun'	陽台/阳台 sun + platform = 'balcony'

天氣暖和的時候，很多人喜歡在海灘上曬太陽。	天气暖和的时候，很多人喜欢在海滩上晒太阳。
這個房間陽光很好，非常明亮。	这个房间阳光很好，非常明亮。
我爸爸現在在陽台上曬太陽呢。	我爸爸现在在阳台上晒太阳呢。
在中國，最熱鬧的是春節，不是陽曆新年。	在中国，最热闹的是春节，不是阳历新年。

Modern Traditional Form						Modern Simplified Form					
陽	陽	陽	陽	陽	陽	阳	阳	阳	阳	阳	阳
陽	陽	陽	陽	陽	陽						

陽					阳			

雨 (yǔ)

yǔ	Ancient Form	Later Form	Modern Form
rain			雨
xiàyǔ			下雨

雨 is a pictographic character. It is a sketch of raindrops falling from the sky. 一, at the top, represents the sky, and the dots represent raindrops. 雨 appears in compound words related to 'rain.' For example:

雨季 rain + season = 'rainy season'	雨水 rain + water = 'rainwater'
雨傘/雨伞 rain + umbrella = 'umbrella'	雷雨 thunder + rain = 'thunderstorm'

中國南方有乾季和雨季。	中国南方有干季和雨季。
今年北京的雨水特別多。	今年北京的雨水特别多。
夏天的時候，我們這裡常常有雷雨。	夏天的时候，我们这里常常有雷雨。
在夏威夷，人們出門的時候習慣帶雨傘。	在夏威夷，人们出门的时候习惯带雨伞。

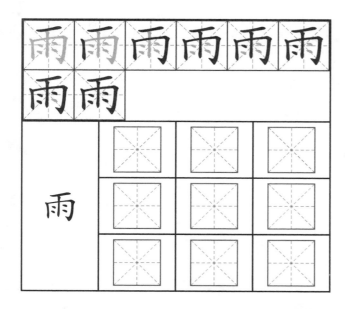

xuě	Ancient Form	Later Form	Modern Form
snow	⅏	雪	雪
xiàxuě			下雪

雪 means 'snow.' The ancient form of 雪 consists of some dots, which represent rain, and two featherlike parts that represent snowflakes. The dots were later replaced with the character 雨 (*yǔ*, 'rain'), and the two featherlike parts were replaced with ヨ. 雪 appears in compound words related to 'snow.' For example:

雪人 snow + person = 'snowman'	雪山 snow + mountain = 'snow-capped mountain'
雪花 snow + flower = 'snowflake'	冰天雪地 ice + sky + snow + ground = 'a world of ice and snow'

這裡每年冬天都會下雪，每次下雪我和爸爸都會做雪人。	这里每年冬天都会下雪，每次下雪我和爸爸都会做雪人。
我們這裡有很多山，到冬天就變成了雪山，很多人來滑雪。	我们这里有很多山，到冬天就变成了雪山，很多人来滑雪。
這裡是中國最北的地方，冬季很長，幾個月都是冰天雪地的，非常冷。	这里是中国最北的地方，冬季很长，几个月都是冰天雪地的，非常冷。
下雪了，好大的雪花，真漂亮。	下雪了，好大的雪花，真漂亮。

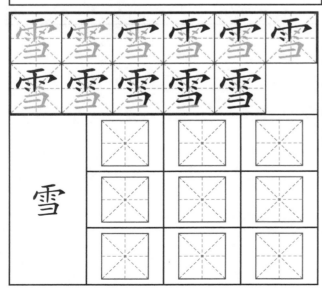

如 (*rú*)

rú	Ancient Form	Later Form	Modern Form
as; like			如
bǐrú			比如

如 is formed with 女 (*nǚ*, 'woman') and 口 (*kǒu*, 'mouth'). In the ancient form, there is a 女 kneeling down to a 口. Confucianism stressed that a girl should listen to her father's teachings before she is married, and she should listen to her husband's commands after she is married. The original meaning of 如 was 'to follow; to comply.' Later, 如 came to mean 'as; according to.' 如 usually appears in compound words that mean 'as; like.' For example:

一見如故／一见如故 one + see + as + old = 'feel like old friends at the first meeting'	如同 as + same = 'like'
心口如一 heart + mouth + as + one = 'frank'	如今 as + today = 'nowadays'

我喜歡水上運動，比如沖浪、游泳。	我喜欢水上运动，比如冲浪、游泳。
他和小王如同一家人。	他和小王如同一家人。
如今的中國人，家家都有了電視、電話。	如今的中国人，家家都有了电视、电话。
我和他一見如故，我覺得他也是一個心口如一的人。	我和他一见如故，我觉得他也是一个心口如一的人。

晴 (*qíng*)

qíng	Later Form	Modern Form
fine, clear (of weather)	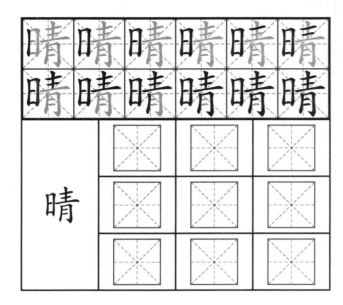	晴
qíngtiān		晴天

The modern form of 晴 is formed with 日 (*rì*, 'sun') and 青 (*qīng*, 'blue'). Both 日 and 青 are radicals, so 晴 indicates a sunny day with blue skies. 青 is also a phonetic component. There are very few compound words with 晴. 晴天 is the only one that is commonly used.

今天是一個大晴天，很多人在外面玩。	今天是一个大晴天，很多人在外面玩。
雨過天晴了，空氣很新鮮。	雨过天晴了，空气很新鲜。
北京秋天的時候，晴天最多。	北京秋天的时候，晴天最多。
今天早上天氣很陰，中午天就晴了。	今天早上天气很阴，中午天就晴了。

曬/晒 (shài)

shài	Later Form	Modern Traditional Form	Modern Simplified Form
expose to sunlight; dry in the air	曬	曬	晒
shài tàiyáng		曬太陽	晒太阳

曬/晒 has 日 (*rì*, 'sun') on the left as the radical. The right part of the later and modern traditional forms is 鹿 (*lù*, 'deer') and antlers. The idea behind the character is that ancient people lived by hunting. After they ate the deer's meat, they would leave its skin in the sun to dry for clothing. 曬/晒 therefore means 'expose to sunlight; dry in the sun.' 曬/晒 usually stands alone and is not used in compound words.

今天天氣真好，我們出去曬太陽吧。	今天天气真好，我们出去晒太阳吧。
你出門別忘了用防曬霜。	你出门别忘了用防晒霜。
中國女孩子特別注意防曬。	中国女孩子特别注意防晒。
中國人喜歡在太陽下曬衣服。	中国人喜欢在太阳下晒衣服。

Modern Traditional Form	Modern Simplified Form
曬 曬	晒 晒 晒 晒 晒 晒 晒 晒 晒 晒
曬	晒

Copyright © 2012 by Yale University and China International Publishing Group

sǎn	Later Form	Modern Traditional Form	Modern Simplified Form
umbrella		傘	伞
yǔsǎn		雨傘	雨伞

The later form of this character represents the original meaning of 傘/伞. It was an umbrella carried by a guard of honor in a ceremony. The modern form of 傘/伞 is a pictographic character. It has 人 on top to represent the canopy of an open umbrella. The bottom part of the character represents the stretchers and shaft of an umbrella.

外面雨不大，你不用打傘。	外面雨不大，你不用打伞。
夏天太曬的時候，女孩子常常用陽傘。	夏天太晒的时候，女孩子常常用阳伞。
我買了雨傘後，一直沒下雨。	我买了雨伞后，一直没下雨。
我孩子下雨時總是打著傘出去，回來時雨傘就不見了。	我孩子下雨时总是打着伞出去，回来时雨伞就不见了。

Modern Traditional Form	Modern Simplified Form
傘 傘 傘 傘 傘 傘	伞 伞 伞 伞 伞 伞
傘 傘 傘 傘 傘 傘	
傘	伞

決/决 (jué)

jué	Later Form	Modern Traditional Form	Modern Simplified Form
decide	𣲰	決	决
juédìng		決定	决定

The original meaning of 決/决 was 'open a dam and allow water to flow.' 水/氵 (*shuǐ*, 'water'), on the left, is the radical, which indicates that the whole character is related to water. 夬 (*jué*, 'to separate'), on the right, is the phonetic component. Later, 決/决 came to mean 'differentiate; make a judgment.' From this meaning, 決/决 is used to mean 'make a decision.' Why does the modern simplified form use 冫 instead of 氵? We don't know, but we can put it this way: 冫 means 'ice,' and making a decision is like breaking ice. Using 冫 seems more determined. 決/决 appears in many compound words that mean 'decide; make a judgment.' For example:

決心/决心 decide + heart = 'determination'	決定/决定 decide + stable = 'decide; determine'
公決/公决 public + decide = 'joint decision'	解決/解决 untie + decide = 'settle; resolve'

這個週末是個大晴天，我們決定去郊遊。	这个周末是个大晴天，我们决定去郊游。
他下定決心, 要學好中文。	他下定决心，要学好中文。
我有個問題不知道怎麼解決，想聽聽你的看法。	我有个问题不知道怎么解决，想听听你的看法。
這件事需要大家討論公決。	这件事需要大家讨论公决。

Modern Traditional Form	Modern Simplified Form
决 决 决 决 决 决	决 决 决 决 决 决
决	

决				决			

定 (dìng)

dìng	Later Form	Modern Form
stable; fixed; decide	定	定
juédìng		決定/决定

The top part of 定 is 宀, the radical, which means the roof of a building. Some say that the bottom part is 正 (*zhèng*), the phonetic component, whereas others say the bottom part is 足 (*zú*, 'foot'), another radical. 宀 and 足 together suggest that one has returned home from traveling and things are settled. 定 usually appears in compound words related to 'decide; stable; fixed.' For example:

定時 / 定时 fixed + time = 'fixed time'	一定 whole + fixed = 'surely; certainly'
安定 peaceful; quiet + stable = 'stable'	決定/决定 decide + decide = 'decide; determine'

他每天定時起床、看書、上網。	他每天定时起床、看书、上网。
我決定今年冬天帶孩子們去滑雪。	我决定今年冬天带孩子们去滑雪。
秋天去北京，你一定要去爬香山。	秋天去北京，你一定要去爬香山。
那件事發生以後，公司裡人心很不安定。	那件事发生以后，公司里人心很不安定。

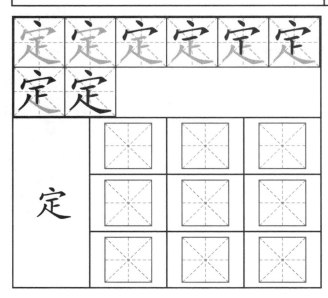

風/风 (fēng)

fēng	Ancient Form	Later Form	Modern Traditional Form	Modern Simplified Form
wind	義	鳳	風	风
guāfēng			颳風	刮风

The ancient Chinese didn't know that wind is created by air movement. They thought wind came from the sky, and it was the reason why birds could fly. Therefore, the ancient form of the character for wind was a sketch of a big flying bird. The later form has 气 (qì, 'air') on top and 虫 (chóng, 'insect') inside 气. The idea was that when wind blows, insects will fly with the wind and spread. The top part of the modern forms uses part of the character 凡 (fán) as a phonetic component. Later, 風/风 came to mean 'something very influential and easily and quickly disseminated as if airborne,' such as news, habits, ways of doing things, and social customs. 風/风 appears in compound words related to 'wind' or 'habits and ways of doing things.' For example:

季風/季风 season + wind = 'monsoon'	風味/风味 habits and ways of doing things + taste = 'special flavor; local color'
風土人情/风土人情 habits and ways of doing things + land + people + feeling = 'local conditions and customs'	耳邊風/耳边风 ear + side + wind = 'a puff of wind passing the ear; unheeded advice'

今天刮大風，所以我決定不出去看什麼風景了，就待在家裡休息。	今天刮大风，所以我决定不出去看什么风景了，就待在家里休息。
我從北京回來的時候，買了一些北京風味的小吃。	我从北京回来的时候，买了一些北京风味的小吃。
只有在一個地方住上一段時間，才能真的了解那裡的風土人情。	只有在一个地方住上一段时间，才能真的了解那里的风土人情。
你不要再把媽媽的話當耳邊風。	你不要再把妈妈的话当耳边风。

Modern Traditional Form	Modern Simplified Form
風 風 風 風 風 風 風 風 風	风 风 风 风

風				风			

景 (*jǐng*)

jǐng	Later Form	Modern Form
scenery; view; situation	景	景
fēngjǐng		風景/风景

景 originally meant 'sunlight.' How does one express sunlight? Sunlight causes shadows, so the later form of 景 is formed with two similar parts, one on top of the other. In ancient Chinese, 景 also meant 'shadow.' In modern Chinese, 'shadow' is represented by a new character, 影 (*yǐng*), which was created by adding 彡 ('sunshine') to 景. The modern form uses 日 (*rì*, 'sun') as the radical and 京 (*jīng*) as the phonetic component. Memorable scenery usually has the sun as part of it. In this sense, 景 came to mean 'scenery; view.' From 'scenery,' 景 was extended to mean 'situation; condition.' 景 usually appears in compound words related to 'scenery' or 'situation.' For example:

風景/风景 wind + scenery = 'landscape'	景色 scenery + color = 'scene'
前景 front; forward + situation = 'prospect'	景點/景点 scenery + spot = 'sightseeing spot'

美國黃石公園 (Yellowstone) 的風景每個季節都很漂亮。	美国黄石公园 (Yellowstone) 的风景每个季节都很漂亮。
冬天爬香山，景色美，空氣也新鮮。	冬天爬香山，景色美，空气也新鲜。
北京有很多景點，你去過哪幾個？	北京有很多景点，你去过哪几个？
這是一個大公司，你好好做，前景會很好的。	这是一个大公司，你好好做，前景会很好的。

景	景	景	景	景	景
景	景	景	景	景	景

景			

內 / 内 (nèi)

nèi	Ancient Form	Later Form	Modern Traditional Form	Modern Simplified Form
in; inside; internal	冈	内	內	内
guónèi			國內	国内

In the ancient and later forms, the upper part of the character resembles a cave or a framework of a house. The lower part is 入 (rù, 'to enter'). 'To enter a house or cave' means 'to be inside.' Therefore, 內/内 means 'inside; in.' Its extended meaning is 'internal.' Note that the modern traditional form retains the lower part 入, whereas the modern simplified form changes it into 人 (rén, 'person'). Can you tell the difference between 入 and 人? 內/内 usually appears in compound words related to 'inside; internal.' For example:

內傷 / 内伤 internal + damage = 'internal injury'	內衣 / 内衣 inside + cloth = 'underwear'
國內 / 国内 nation + internal = 'domestic'	內向 / 内向 inside + direction = 'introverted'

中國人以前只在國內旅遊，現在越來越多的人開始到國外旅遊了。	中国人以前只在国内旅游，现在越来越多的人开始到国外旅游了。
孩子從自行車上掉下來後，他擔心 (dānxīn, 'worry') 孩子有內傷，送孩子去醫院了。	孩子从自行车上掉下来后，他担心 (dānxīn, 'worry') 孩子有内伤，送孩子去医院了。
天晴的時候，她喜歡在後院曬衣服，內衣曬一曬，穿了對身體好。	天晴的时候，她喜欢在后院晒衣服，内衣晒一晒，穿了对身体好。
我的兒子比女兒內向很多。	我的儿子比女儿内向很多。

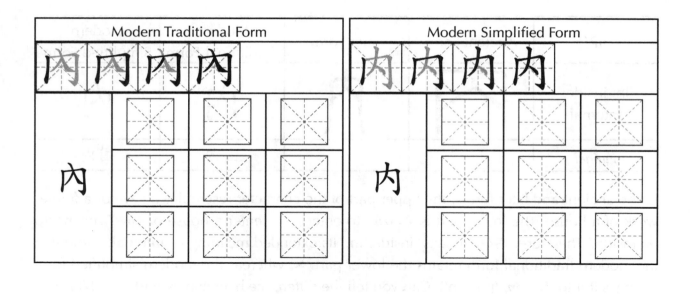

Modern Traditional Form				Modern Simplified Form			

The sentences below are inspired by the contents of Unit 20 and contain all the new characters required for writing as well as others. Read and reread until fluent, covering the English as you read. Then cover the English and try to reproduce the Chinese equivalents orally. Do this exercise before beginning to practice writing.

很多外國學生覺得漢字很難學。 很多外国学生觉得汉字很难学。	Lots of foreign students feel that Chinese characters are hard to learn.
老師要我們把不懂的單詞抄寫下來。 老师要我们把不懂的单词抄写下来。	The teacher asks us to copy down the words we don't understand.
這個句子太長了，很難懂。 这个句子太长了，很难懂。	This sentence is too long; it's hard to understand.
學習語言就跟學習樂器一樣，要慢慢來。 学习语言就跟学习乐器一样，要慢慢来。	Learning a language is like learning a musical instrument; you have to take your time learning.
我們念中學的時候，要背誦古文。如果背 　　錯了，會被罰。 我们念中学的时候，要背诵古文。如果背 　　错了，会被罚。	When we were in high school, we had to recite classic Chinese prose. If we made mistakes, we'd be punished.
他下班以後，去一所中文學校學習中文。 他下班以后，去一所中文学校学习中文。	After work, he learns Chinese in a Chinese language school.
中文的拼音剛開始學比較難，可是習慣了 　　以後，其實並沒有那麼難。 中文的拼音刚开始学比较难，可是习惯了 　　以后，其实并没有那么难。	Chinese pinyin is relatively hard at first; however, after you get used to it, it's actually not that difficult.

Some More Thoughts about Chinese Dictionaries

Assuming you have completed the dictionary exercises in Unit 20 of your *Encounters* textbook, you now have a pretty good idea of how to look up a Chinese character, either by its pinyin spelling (if you know the pronunciation) or by its radical and remaining strokes (if you don't know the pronunciation). You also have an appreciation for just how different the processes are—one can be as quick and foolproof as when you look up an English word in your dictionary, and the other can be a rather time-consuming and frustrating process. You have practiced locating the radical in a character, consulting the chart of radicals, counting the remaining strokes, and ultimately finding the character you seek. It's now time to introduce you to other dictionaries on the market that can help you as you continue to learn Chinese. We divide them into two types, depending on the immediate needs of the situation when you look up new characters or words.

(1) Let's say you're in China and you hear the following sentence: *Zuótiān wǎnshang wǒ gēn péngyou qù kàn yí bù diànyǐng, shì ge kǒngbù diànyǐng. Wǒ hěn bù xǐhuan.* You want to know what *kǒngbù* means. You don't know the characters, so how do you do the quickest lookup?

Use the *ABC Chinese-English English-Chinese Dictionary* (pocket version), edited by John DeFrancis, or one like it. You can simply look up the word by its pinyin spelling, and you will find its meaning—'terror' > *kǒngbù diànyǐng* > 'horror movie.' In fact, you will also find an example sentence, parts of speech, tones, Chinese characters (in both forms), and other useful information.

Another dictionary similar to the DeFrancis *ABC* is *Langenscheidt's Pocket Dictionary* (Chinese to English and English to Chinese). It is not quite as comprehensive as the *ABC*, but it is still very useful and a bit more pocket sized.

Still another is the *Oxford Starter Chinese Dictionary*, which has lots of handy guides for the Chinese beginner but is far less comprehensive than the other two examples.

(2) Now let's say you're reading a short descriptive piece that goes like this:

我朋友在中國是一位非常有名的作家，是個北京人。他寫了幾本小説和雜文。	我朋友在中國是一位非常有名的作家，是个北京人。他写了几本小说和杂文。

You don't know the meaning of the last word nor can you pronounce the next-to-last character (雜/杂). Context suggests that the word has something to do with writing, but what precisely does 雜文/杂文 mean?

Well, by now, you should know the drill. Find the radical in the radical chart that directs you to the appropriate page in the radical index, count the remaining strokes, and then find 雜 or 杂 (depending on which form of text you're reading, simplified or traditional) under the remaining strokes listings. There you will find the exact page reference for 雜/杂. Turn to that page and find 雜/杂. The main entry will provide the many usages of *zá* (now you can pronounce it!) as a single character; below that there will be an alphabetical list of compound words that begin with *zá*. Go down the list, find 雜文/杂文, and now you know its meaning: *záwén* = 'essay'

So which dictionary do we recommend for this kind of lookup—when you can't pronounce a character or word? The best is the award-winning *The Contemporary Chinese Dictionary* [Chinese-English edition], Foreign Language Teaching and Research Press, Beijing, 2002.

Now let's suppose you can pronounce 雜文/杂文 but have forgotten its meaning. Well, modern Chinese dictionaries are arranged by the alpha-pinyin spelling of single characters. You need only to flip to '*za*,' find 雜/杂, look down the list, find 雜文/杂文, and presto! You have your answer. (Of course, in cases like these, you can also use the *ABC* dictionary.)

難/难 (*nán*)

nán	Later Form	Modern Traditional Form	Modern Simplified Form
difficult; hard	難	難	难
Hànzì hěn nán xué.		漢字很難學。	汉字很难学。

難/难 originally meant one type of bird. 隹 (*zhuī*), on the right, is the radical, meaning 'small bird.' Later, 難/难 was borrowed to mean 'difficult; hard.' The left part of the traditional form is 堇, which is a phonetic component. However, it is no longer reliable, so the modern simplified form replaces it with 又 (*yòu*). Here's a memory aid: 又 often means 'hand' in a character. Is it difficult to catch a bird (隹) with your bare hands? 難/难 appears in many compound words related to 'difficult' or 'hard.' For example:

難題/难题 difficult + question; problem = 'difficult problem'	難看/难看 hard + look = 'ugly'
難聽/难听 hard + listen = 'unpleasant to hear'	難過/难过 hard + pass = 'feel sad; have a hard time'

他覺得漢語的聲調很難掌握。	他觉得汉语的声调很难掌握。
小張碰到一個難題，不知道大學畢業後是上研究生院還是工作。	小张碰到一个难题，不知道大学毕业后是上研究生院还是工作。
我唱歌很難聽，跳舞很難看，你就別叫我給大家唱歌、跳舞了。	我唱歌很难听，跳舞很难看，你就别叫我给大家唱歌、跳舞了。
他怎麼了？為什麼看起來那麼難過？	他怎么了？为什么看起来那么难过？

Modern Traditional Form	Modern Simplified Form

難 難 難 難 難 難
難 難 難 難 難 難
難 難 難 難 難 難
難

难 难 难 难 难 难
难 难 难 难

難

难

所 (*suǒ*)

suǒ	Later Form	Modern Form
place; (an auxiliary word)	所	所
suǒyǐ		所以

所 has 戶 (*hù*, 'door') on the left and 斤 (*jīn*, 'ax') on the right. The original meaning of 所 was 'the sound from cutting trees.' Trees are cut for timber to make a building, so 所 was extended to mean 'a place for living, offices, or institutes.' Along the same line, 所 is also used as a measure word for buildings and institutes, for example: 一所學校/一所学校 ('a school') and 一所房子 ('a house'). Together with 以, 所以 is a conjuction word, meaning 'therefore; as a result.' In modern Chinese, 所 is often used as an auxiliary word before a verb to denote the object of an action. You will learn this when your Chinese reaches a more advanced level. 所 appears in compound words related to 'place' or as an auxiliary word. For example:

廁所/厕所 toilet + place = 'restroom; bathroom'	無所不能/无所不能 no + auxiliary word + not + can = 'omnipotent'
住所 to live + place = 'dwelling place; residence'	無所事事/无所事事 no + auxiliary word + to be engaged in + things = 'be occupied with nothing; be at loose ends'

這所房子雖然很大，可是只有一個廁所。	这所房子虽然很大，可是只有一个厕所。
這個人無所不能，所以他有很多朋友。	这个人无所不能，所以他有很多朋友。
我從飛機場接到小王後，就直接把他送到住所。	我从飞机场接到小王后，就直接把他送到住所。
大學畢業後，他找不到工作，呆在家裡無所事事。	大学毕业后，他找不到工作，呆在家里无所事事。

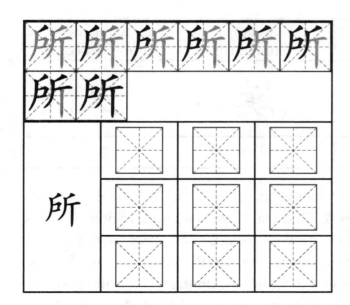

漢/汉 (hàn)

hàn	Later Form	Modern Traditional Form	Modern Simplified Form
of the Chinese people or language	𤁉	漢	汉
Hànzì		漢字	汉字

漢語/汉语 ('Chinese language'), 漢字/汉字 ('Chinese character'), and 漢人/汉人 ('the Han people; the Hans') all originated in 漢朝/汉朝 ('the Han Dynasty'). In addition, 漢朝/汉朝 acquired its name from 漢水/汉水 ('the Han River') because 漢水/汉水 rises from the capital area of the Han Dynasty. 漢/汉 originally meant 'the Han River.' 氵, on the left, is the radical, indicating the whole character is related to water. 堇, on the right, is the phonetic component, but it is no longer reliable. Remember the character 難/难? 漢/汉 in modern Chinese usually means 'Chinese people' or 'Chinese language.' Colloquially, 漢/汉 also means 'man.' For example:

漢學/汉学 Chinese people + study = 'Sinology'	漢語/汉语 Chinese language + language = 'Chinese language'
男子漢/男子汉 man + suffix + man = 'a manly man'	好漢/好汉 good + man = 'true man; hero'

他漢語聲調説得不錯，可是漢字寫得不好。	他汉语声调说得不错，可是汉字写得不好。
這個美國學生是研究漢學的，漢語説得非常好。	这个美国学生是研究汉学的，汉语说得非常好。
是男子漢就不要怕苦怕累。	是男子汉就不要怕苦怕累。
在我眼裡，我的朋友個個都是好漢。	在我眼里，我的朋友个个都是好汉。

Modern Traditional Form	Modern Simplified Form
漢 漢 漢 漢 漢 漢 漢 漢 漢 漢 漢 漢 漢 漢	汉 汉 汉 汉 汉

漢				汉			

言 (yán)

yán	Ancient Form	Later Form	Modern Form
words; language; to say			言
yǔyán			語言/语言

言 originally meant 'to speak.' Later, it was extended to mean 'words; language.' 言 has 口 (kǒu, 'mouth') at the bottom as the radical, indicating 言 is related to mouth. The ancient form is a sketch of a tongue extending from a mouth. Memory aid for the modern form? How about sound waves above a mouth? 言 appears in compound words related to 'words,' 'speech,' or 'to say.' For example:

食言 to eat + words = 'break one's word'	美言 beautiful + to say = 'put in a good word for someone'
名言 fame + words = 'famous sayings'	冷言冷語/冷言冷语 cold + to say + cold + to talk = 'sarcastic comment'

漢語是一個有聲調的語言。	汉语是一个有声调的语言。
他說他會幫我，他不會食言的。	他说他会帮我，他不会食言的。
我喜歡那個女孩子，請你在她面前為我美言幾句。	我喜欢那个女孩子，请你在她面前为我美言几句。
聽了他的冷言冷語，我很難過。	听了他的冷言冷语，我很难过。

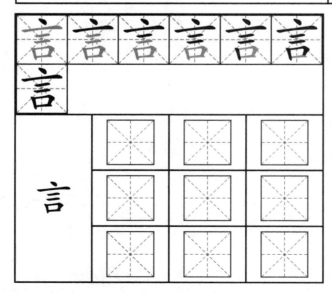

習 / 习 (xí)

xí	Ancient Form	Later Form	Modern Traditional Form	Modern Simplified Form
to practice			習	习
liànxí			練習	练习

The top part of the ancient form is 羽 (*yǔ*, 'feather'), and the bottom part is 日 (*rì*, 'sun'). The original meaning of 習/习 was a bird learning to fly in the sky. Later, 習/习 was extended to mean 'to practice,' 'to exercise,' 'become familiar with,' and 'be used to.' It is also used to mean 'habit' or 'custom.' 習/习 usually appears in compound words related to 'practice' or 'habit.' For example:

學習/学习 learn + practice = 'study'	習慣/习惯 be used to + usual = 'habit; custom'
自習/自习 self + practice = (of students) 'study by oneself in scheduled time or free time'	習性/习性 habit + nature = 'behavior'

學習外語需要很多練習。	学习外语需要很多练习。
他習慣走到哪裡都帶著他的字典。	他习惯走到哪里都带着他的字典。
學生自習的時間都習慣去圖書館。	学生自习的时间都习惯去图书馆。
幾個星期後，他就了解了他養的這條狗的習性。	几个星期后，他就了解了他养的这条狗的习性。

Modern Traditional Form						Modern Simplified Form		
習	習	習	習	習	習	习	习	习
習	習	習	習	習				

習				习			

慣/惯 (*guàn*)

guàn	Later Form	Modern Traditional Form	Modern Simplified Form
habitual; be used to; to spoil	遺	慣	惯
xíguàn		習慣	习惯

The original form of 慣/惯 is 貫/贯, which originally meant 'a string of 1,000 coins' in ancient times. The bottom part is 貝/贝 (*bèi*, 'cowrie; money'). The top part is 毌, which is a cross stringing things together. Later, 貫/贯 was extended to mean 'pass through.' Then 貫/贯 was loaned to mean 'habit.' In modern Chinese, 'habit' is represented by a new character, 慣/惯, which was created by adding 忄 (*xīn*, 'heart') to 貫/贯. The idea is that 慣/惯 is a habit of the heart. In compound words, 慣/惯 usually means 'habitual.' A bad habit is the consequence of spoiling or indulging. Therefore, 慣/惯 in some compound words means 'to spoil' or 'to indulge.' For example:

慣偷/惯偷 habitual + to steal = 'hardened thief'	嬌慣/娇惯 sweet and charming + to spoil = 'coddle; pamper'
慣用/惯用 habitual + use = 'habitually practice'	看不慣/看不惯 look + not + habitual = 'dislike'

很多中國人習慣喝熱茶，不習慣喝冰水。	很多中国人习惯喝热茶，不习惯喝冰水。
父母嬌慣孩子現在在中國很常見。	父母娇惯孩子现在在中国很常见。
我看不慣他那樣罵人。	我看不惯他那样骂人。
這是他慣用的偷錢的方法。	这是他惯用的偷钱的方法。

Modern Traditional Form						Modern Simplified Form					
慣	慣	慣	慣	慣	慣	惯	惯	惯	惯	惯	惯
慣	慣	慣	慣	慣	慣	惯	惯	惯	惯	惯	
慣	慣										

慣				惯			

慢 (màn)

màn	Later Form	Modern Form
slow; sluggish; disrespectful	慢	慢
Qǐng mànman shuō.		請慢慢説。/ 请慢慢说。

The original meaning of 慢 was 'arrogant; to despise.' 忄 is the radical, indicating the whole character is related to heart. 曼 (*màn*) on the right is the phonetic component. When one is arrogant toward or despises others, one tends to be slow to respond or react to them. Therefore, the meaning of 慢 was extended to mean 'slow; tardy.' 曼 as a phonetic component appears in quite a few characters. Two of the most useful ones include 饅/馒 (*mán*, 'steamed bun') and 漫 (màn, 'overflow; casual'). 慢 appears in compound words related to 'slow' or 'disrespectful.' For example:

快慢 quick + slow = 'speed'	輕慢/轻慢 light + disrespectful = 'treat someone without proper respect'
慢性 slow + nature = 'chronic'	慢待 disrespectful + treat = 'slight'

開始學中文的時候，不習慣聲調，要慢慢説。	开始学中文的时候，不习惯声调，要慢慢说。
他有慢性病，常常不能來上班。	他有慢性病，常常不能来上班。
中文進步的快慢和學習時間的多少有關係。	中文进步的快慢和学习时间的多少有关系。
在我們的飯店裡，一定不能慢待客人。	在我们的饭店里，一定不能慢待客人。

慢	慢	慢	慢	慢	慢
慢	慢	慢	慢	慢	慢
慢	慢				

慢			

背 (*bèi*)

bèi	Ancient Form	Later Form	Modern Form
memorize; the back (of something)	仆	𦝠	背
bèisòng			背誦 / 背诵

北 is the original form of the character 背, meaning 'back of the body.' Its ancient form is a sketch of two people back to back. Later, 北 was more often used to mean 'north.' The original meaning of 'back of the body' was represented by a new character, 背, which was created by adding 月 (*yuè*, 'moon') to 北. 月 is equivalent to 肉 (*ròu*, 'flesh; meat') when used as a radical in characters related to the body, such as the following characters: 胖 (*pàng*, 'fat'), 肚 (*dù*, 'stomach'), 臉/脸 (*liǎn*, 'face'). From the meaning 'back of the body,' 背 was later extended to mean 'back of an object' and 'carry on one's back.' When you study and try to memorize something, you sometimes hide the book or notebook behind your back. Therefore, 背 was extended to mean 'memorize.' Note that when 背 means 'carry on one's back,' 背 is pronounced with the first tone—*bēi*. 背 usually appears in compound words related to 'back of the body or an object' or 'memorize.' For example:

手背 hand + back = 'the back of hand'	背書 / 背书 to memorize + book = 'recite a lesson from memory'
背包 back + bag = 'backpack'	背影 back + shadow; reflection = 'a view of someone's back'

學外語常常要背很多東西。	学外语常常要背很多东西。
我的背包裡有很多書。	我的背包里有很多书。
我小的時候，我媽媽總是讓我背書。	我小的时候，我妈妈总是让我背书。
小孩子喜歡在手背上畫畫、寫字。	小孩子喜欢在手背上画画、写字。

背	背	背	背	背	背
背	背	背			

背			

抄 (chāo)

chāo	Later Form	Modern Form
copy; transcribe	 	抄
chāoxiě		抄寫／抄写

抄 has 扌/手 (*shǒu*, 'hand'), on the left, as the radical, indicating the whole character is related to hand action. 少 (*shǎo*), on the right, is the phonetic component. The later form had 金 (*jīn*, 'metal') on the left as the radical. This is because the original meaning of 抄 was 'to seize' or 'to take up with a fork.' The radical 金 indicated the whole character was a type of metal tool. The modern form replaces 金 with 扌, emphasizing the 'hand action.' To copy or transcribe is to take another's work, much like seizing. Therefore, the meaning of 抄 was extended to 'copy' and 'transcribe.' 抄 usually appears in compound words related to 'copy' or 'transcribe.' For example:

抄寫／抄写 transcribe + write = 'copy down'	抄錄／抄录 transcribe + record = 'make a copy of; copy down'
開始學中文的時候，抄寫生詞和課文很有用。	开始学中文的时候，抄写生词和课文很有用。
我看完了那本書，而且抄錄了一些很漂亮的句子。	我看完了那本书，而且抄录了一些很漂亮的句子。

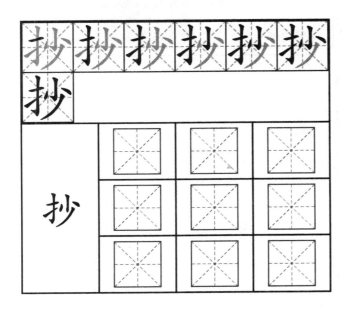

把 (bǎ)

bǎ	Later Form	Modern Form
(used before a direct object and followed by a transitive verb); to hold	𢪛	把
Wǒ bǎ shū jiè gěi péngyou le.		我把書借給朋友了。 我把书借给朋友了。

把 has 扌/手 (*shǒu*, 'hand'), on the left, as the radical, indicating the whole character is related to hand action. 巴 (*bā*), on the right, is the phonetic component. The original meaning of 把 was 'to hold.' To hold something is to do something with it. Therefore, in colloquial Chinese, 把 is often used in a *bǎ* construction to imply a stronger sense that something is being done to the object. From the original meaning of 'to hold,' the meaning of 把 was extended to 'to guard' and 'a handle.' When 把 appears in a compound word, it means 'to hold,' 'to guard,' or 'a handle.' For example:

把門/把门 to guard + gate = 'guard the entrance (gate)'	把手 to hold + hand = 'knob; handle'
車把/车把 vehicle + handle = 'handlebar (of a bicycle, motorcycle, etc.)'	把玩 to hold + to play = 'hold and appreciate'

中文老師讓我把課文抄寫下來。	中文老师让我把课文抄写下来。
我把我的字典借給了同學。	我把我的字典借给了同学。
在中國，每個學校都有把門的人。	在中国，每个学校都有把门的人。
我得給我的自行車換個新車把。	我得给我的自行车换个新车把。

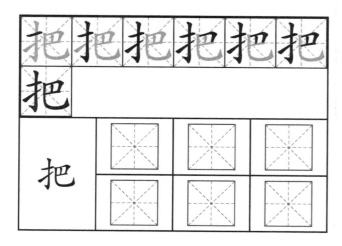

錯/错 (cuò)

cuò	Later Form	Modern Traditional Form	Modern Simplified Form
wrong; mistake; error; fault	錯	錯	错
méicuò		没錯	没错

錯/错 has 金/钅 (*jīn*, 'metal'), on the left, as the radical, indicating the whole character is related to metal. 昔, on the right, used to be the phonetic component, but it is not reliable at all in modern Chinese. The original meaning of 錯/错 was 'to inlay with gold, silver, etc.' Later, it was extended to mean 'interlaced' and 'interleaving.' 'Interleaving' means two things can't combine or unite. Therefore, the meaning of 錯/错 was extended to 'something wrong that doesn't conform to the customs or regulations of society.' 錯/错 usually appears in compound words related to 'interlaced' or 'mistake,' but you will more often see it as a verbal suffix meaning 'to do the verb wrongly' (寫錯/写错). For example:

交錯/交错 cross + interlaced = 'interlaced'	錯怪/错怪 mistake + to blame = 'blame somebody wrongly'
錯過/错过 interlaced + pass = 'miss; lose'	認錯/认错 admit + mistake = 'acknowledge one's mistake'

今天的小考，我寫錯了兩個漢字。	今天的小考，我写错了两个汉字。
站在高高的教學樓上，你能看到這個城市交錯的公路。	站在高高的教学楼上，你能看到这个城市交错的公路。
不要錯過這個很好的工作機會。	不要错过这个很好的工作机会。
今天早上我錯怪你了，現在我向你認錯。	今天早上我错怪你了，现在我向你认错。

Modern Traditional Form	Modern Simplified Form
錯 錯 錯 錯 錯 錯 錯 錯 錯 錯 錯 錯 錯 錯 錯 錯	错 错 错 错 错 错 错 错 错 错 错 错 错

錯			

错			

罰/罚 *(fá)*

fá	Later Form	Modern Traditional Form	Modern Simplified Form
penalize; punish	罰	罰	罚
Lǎoshī fá xuésheng chāo kèwén.		老師罰學生抄課文。	老师罚学生抄课文。

罰/罚 means 'to penalize; to punish.' Regarding the top part, ㎜, there are two different explanations. Some say that ㎜ means 'net,' which indicates 'to arrest' or 'to capture.' By contrast, others say that ㎜ is the top part of 罪 (*zuì*, 'sin; crime'). The bottom left part 言/讠 (*yán*, 'speech') indicates 'trial.' 刀/刂 (*dāo*, 'knife') indicates 'to punish.' 罰/罚 usually appears in compound words related to 'penalize' or 'punish.' For example:

罰酒/罚酒 punish + wine = 'be made to drink as a forfeit'	罰球/罚球 punish + ball = 'free throw'
罰金/罚金 penalize + gold = 'fine'	認罰/认罚 admit + penalty; punishment = 'take punishment'
我寫錯了兩個字，老師罰我每個字抄寫10次。	我写错了两个字，老师罚我每个字抄写10次。
他開車太快了，警察給他了一張罰單，得交120塊罰金。	他开车太快了，警察给他了一张罚单，得交120块罚金。
昨天去朋友家吃飯，我晚到了一個小時，他們要罰酒三杯，我只好認罰。	昨天去朋友家吃饭，我晚到了一个小时，他们要罚酒三杯，我只好认罚。
他得到了三次罰球機會。	他得到了三次罚球机会。

Modern Traditional Form	Modern Simplified Form
罰 罰 罰 罰 罰 罰	罚 罚 罚 罚 罚 罚
罰 罰 罰 罰 罰 罰	罚 罚 罚
罰 罰	

罰				罚			

懂 (dǒng)

dǒng	Later Form	Modern Form
understand; comprehend	懂	懂
Wǒ kànbudǒng Zhōngwén bàozhǐ.		我看不懂中文報紙。/ 我看不懂中文报纸。

懂 means 'to understand; to comprehend.' Ancient Chinese people thought that people used their hearts to think. Therefore, 忄/心 (*xīn*, 'heart'), on the left, is the radical, indicating the whole character is related to heart. 董 (*dǒng*), on the right, is the phonetic component. Note that 董 is formed with 艹 ('grass') on top of 重 (*zhòng*, 'heavy; important'). A memory aid: 重要 ('important') 的事情你一定要懂. 懂 usually stands alone. 懂事 ('know the ropes; know the business') is one commonly used compound word. You will often run into 懂 in resultative verbal expressions, such as 看懂, 看不懂.

這個孩子很懂事。	这个孩子很懂事。
你能看懂中文電視節目嗎？	你能看懂中文电视节目吗？
古文比白話文難懂。	古文比白话文难懂。
要是你聽不懂，就問老師。	要是你听不懂，就问老师。

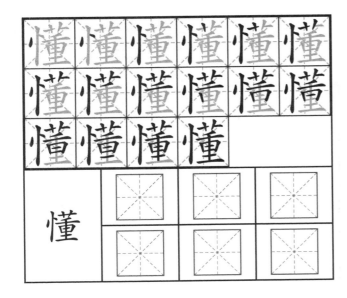

古 (gǔ)

gǔ	Ancient Form	Later Form	Modern Form
ancient	𠮷	古	古
gǔdài			古代

The ancient form of 古 was a vertical stroke passing through two 口 (kǒu, 'mouth'). Later, 古 was formed with 十 (shí, 'ten') and 口. The idea is that the stories of ancient times are passed down by many mouths (people). 古 appears in compound words related to 'ancient' or 'old.' For example:

古畫/古画 old + painting = 'ancient painting'	古老 ancient + old = 'ancient'
古話/古话 old + words = 'old saying'	古人 ancient + person = 'the ancients'

中國的中學生要學習古文。	中国的中学生要学习古文。
他家裡有很多古畫，都很貴。	他家里有很多古画，都很贵。
春節吃餃子是一個古老的習俗。	春节吃饺子是一个古老的习俗。
中國有一句古話，"活到老，學到老。"	中国有一句古话，"活到老，学到老。"

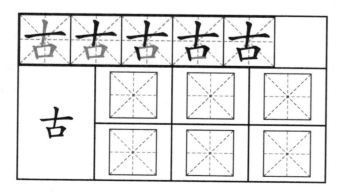

pīn	Later Form	Modern Form
put together; spell (a word)	拼	拼
pīnyīn		拼音

The original meaning of 拼 was 'to put together.' 拼 has 扌/手 (*shǒu*, 'hand'), on the left, as the radical, indicating the whole character is related to hand action. 并 (*bìng*), on the right, is the phonetic component and another signific component. 并 itself looks like two hands put together. 拼 appears in some compound words related to 'put together.' For example:

拼圖/拼图 to put together + picture = 'picture puzzle'	拼讀/拼读 to put together + to read aloud = 'spell out'
拼寫/拼写 to put together + write = 'spell; spelling'	拼盤/拼盘 to put together + tray = 'assorted cold dishes'

學中文，你不能只學拼音不學漢字。	学中文，你不能只学拼音不学汉字。
他會說很好的英文，可是他不會拼寫，也不會拼讀。	他会说很好的英文，可是他不会拼写，也不会拼读。
小孩子都喜歡玩拼圖。	小孩子都喜欢玩拼图。
他在家請客的時候，總是做一個水果拼盤。	他在家请客的时候，总是做一个水果拼盘。

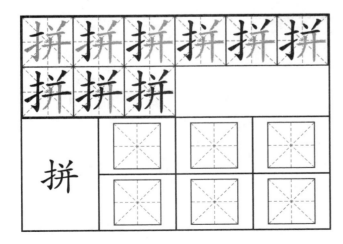

長/长 (*cháng*)

cháng	Ancient Form	Later Form	Modern Traditional Form	Modern Simplified Form
long	丂	镸	長	长
cháng shíjiān			長時間	长时间

In ancient China, people usually didn't have their hair cut very often. Therefore, older people usually had longer hair. The ancient form of 長/长 uses the figure of an elderly person with long hair to express the meaning of 'long.' From the meaning of 'long,' 長/长 was extended to mean 'grow,' and the pronunciation of this meaning is *zhǎng*. 'Grow,' by extension of meaning, also signifies 'elder/senior head (of something),' so you have 家長/家长 (head of the family) and one you know already, 校長/校长 (head of a school; principal). 長/长 (*cháng*) turns up in many compound words related to 'long' or 'length.' For example:

長遠/长远 long + far = 'long-term'	長短/长短 long + short = 'length'
長城/长城 long + town = 'The Great Wall'	長期/长期 long + term = 'long-term'

要學好一門外語，需要長時間的學習和練習。	要学好一门外语，需要长时间的学习和练习。
我還沒有什麼長遠的計劃，只想趕快大學畢業。	我还没有什么长远的计划，只想赶快大学毕业。
這條褲子，長短很合適，可是顏色我不喜歡。	这条裤子，长短很合适，可是颜色我不喜欢。
他是美國人，可是長期在北京工作，所以去長城很多次了。	他是美国人，可是长期在北京工作，所以去长城很多次了。

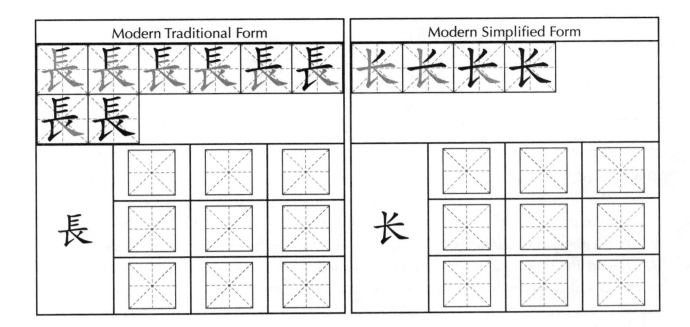

Modern Traditional Form	Modern Simplified Form
長 長 長 長 長 長 長 長	长 长 长 长
長	长

句 (jù)

jù	Ancient Form	Later Form	Modern Form
sentence			句
jùzi			句子

The form of 句 is composed of 口 (kǒu, 'mouth'), representing a square nail and entangled ropes. The original meaning of 句 was 'to bend; to curve.' Later, 句 was extended to mean 'to limit' and 'to divide.' When used for language, 句 refers to sentences, which is the result of dividing long utterances. Gradually, 'sentence' became the primary meaning of 句. 句 appears in compound words related to 'sentence.' It is interesting that 句, which means 'sentence,' also serves as the measure word for sentences: 一句話／一句话. For example:

病句 sick + sentence = 'grammatically wrong sentence'	句法 sentence + law = 'syntax'
分句 divide + sentence = 'clause'	造句 make + sentence = 'sentence making'

你幫我看看，這個句子是不是個病句？	你帮我看看，这个句子是不是个病句？
中文課上，老師常常讓學生做造句練習。	中文课上，老师常常让学生做造句练习。
句法就是研究句子和句子之間的關係。	句法就是研究句子和句子之间的关系。
女兒來信了，只有幾句話。	女儿来信了，只有几句话。

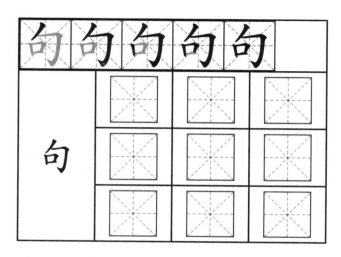

jiē	Later Form	Modern Form
meet; pick up	㨗	接
zài jīchǎng jiē rén		在機場接人 / 在机场接人

接 has 妾 (*qiè*, 'concubine'), on the right, as the phonetic component. 扌/手 (*shǒu*, 'hand'), on the left, is the radical, indicating the whole character is related to hand action. 接 originally meant 'to bring together; to join.' Later, it was extended to mean 'to connect,' 'to meet,' and 'to pick up.' 接 appears in compound words related to 'meet' or 'pick up.' For example:

接機/接机 to pick up + plane = 'pick someone up at the airport'	接見/接见 to meet + to see = 'receive; give an interview to'
交接 to turn over + to pick up = 'hand over and take over (duties of a job, post, etc.)'	接待 to meet + to treat = 'play host to; entertain'

今天老板讓我去接機，接什麼人我還不知道。	今天老板让我去接机，接什么人我还不知道。
我們老板每天都要接見很多人。	我们老板每天都要接见很多人。
今天是我最後一天上班，有很多工作我得交接一下。	今天是我最后一天上班，有很多工作我得交接一下。
新老師已經到了，你出去接待一下。	新老师已经到了，你出去接待一下。

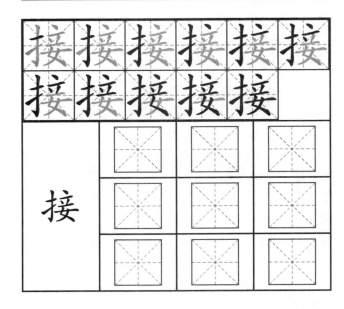

Index I: Characters Arranged by Pinyin

kōng/kòng 空 59
kǔ 苦 40

L

là 辣 41
lǎo 老 24
lè 樂/乐 86
lǐ 禮/礼 65
lǐ 理 154
liáo 聊 203
lóu 樓/楼 136
lǚ 旅 107
lǜ 綠/绿 52

M

má 麻 68
màn 慢 267
mǐ 米 91
miàn 麵/面 93

N

nǎi 奶 87
nán 難/难 256
nèi 內/内 251
niú 牛 42

P

pǎo 跑 120
péng 朋 11
piào 票 228
pīn 拼 279
píng 平 178

Q

qí 騎/骑 218
qì 氣/气 8
qì 汽 225
qiáo 橋/桥 210
qíng 晴 241
qiū 秋 234
qiú 球 106
quán 全 211

R

rán 然 75
ròu 肉 46
rú 如 240

S

sǎn 傘/伞 243
sè 色 53
shài 曬/晒 242
shī 師/师 25
shǐ 始 164
shì 市 51
shì 試/试 150
shì 室 181
shū 蔬 54
shū 書/书 115
shū 舒 176
shù 樹/树 188
sòng 送 74
suān 酸 38
suí 隨/随 99
suǒ 所 258

T

tán 談/谈 7
táo 桃 37
tí 題/题 5
tián 甜 39
tīng 聽/听 110
tīng 廳/厅 143
tōng 通 206
tóng 同 82
tú 圖/图 138

W

wài 外 130
wán 完 163
wàng 望 64
wēi 危 215
wèi 味 45
wèi 衛/卫 197
wèn 問/问 4
wò 臥/卧 179
wù 物 67

X

xī 希 63
xí 習/习 263
xià 夏 233
xiān 鮮/鲜 44
xiǎn 險/险 216
xiāng 香 34
xiào 校 133
xiě 寫/写 27
xīn 新 20
xíng 行 220
xū 需 98
xuǎn 選/选 212
xué 學/学 23
xuě 雪 239

Y

yán 言 262
yáng 陽/阳 236
yīn 音 112
yīng/yìng 應/应 207
yóu 遊/游 108
yǒu 友 12

Index II: Characters Arranged by Number of Strokes

Index III: Comparison of Traditional and Simplified Characters

Some Useful References

Oxford Starter Chinese Dictionary (Oxford University Press, 2000). A very useful dictionary for the beginner in Chinese.

Fundamentals of Chinese Characters, by John Jing-hua Yin (Yale University Press, 2006). A great reference for instruction on recognizing and writing Chinese characters.

Speaking of Chinese, by Raymond Chang and Margaret Seogin Chang (Norton Publishing, 2001). A lively, inspired, and entertaining history of the Chinese language.

How to Be a More Successful Language Learner, by Joan Rubin and Irene Thompson (Heinle and Heinle Publishers, 1994). A great introduction to the strategies and tactics of language learning. A must read before and during your study.

China (Lonely Planet Publications). The best guide to China. Get the latest edition. A must take-along on your trip.

Chinese Characters: A Genealogy and Dictionary, by Rick Harbaugh (Yale University Press, 1998). Very, very useful on origins of characters with a fun website as well: Zhongwen.com.

Name:_____ **Class:**_____

Name:_____ **Class:**_____

Name:_____ **Class:**_____